TABLE OF CONTENTS

Page

ACRONYMS

ACR	Armored Cavalry Regiment
ANSF	Afghan National Security Forces
BPHS	Basic Package of Health Services
CERP	Commander's Emergency Response Program
CJTF-82	Coalition Joint Task Force-82
CSH	Combat Support Hospital
DART	Disaster Assistance Response Team
DOD	Department of Defense
DOS	Department of State
DTP3	Diphtheria, Tetanus, and Pertussis
ePRT	Embedded Provisional Reconstruction Team
FM	Field Manual
ISAF	International Security Assistance Force
JP	Joint Publication
MEDCAP	Medical Civic Action Program
MEDSEM	Medical Seminar
MOH	Ministry of Health
MOPH	Ministry of Public Health
NATO	North Atlantic Treaty Organization
NGO	Non-Governmental Organization
PRT	Provincial Reconstruction Team
UN	United Nations

U.S.   United States

USAID   U.S. Agency for International Development

TABLES

v

CHAPTER 1

INTRODUCTION

Nation-building efforts cannot be successful if adequate attention is not paid to health. Indeed, health can have an important independent impact on nation-building and overall development.

— Seth G. Jones et al.
Securing Health: Lessons from Nation-Building Missions

Overview

For United States (U.S.) Army medical personnel in combat, the expeditious treatment and evacuation of wounded American and allied troops is always the major priority and focus. This certainly applies to the recent conflicts in Iraq and Afghanistan. However, in counterinsurgencies like those in Iraq and Afghanistan, U.S. Army medical personnel have found themselves repeatedly involved to varying degrees with the medical treatment of host nation citizens as a result of collapsed or undeveloped health systems. In addition, Army medical personnel over the last decade have been consistently engaged alongside civilians from a wide variety of organizations, including other U.S. government agencies, Non-Governmental Organizations (NGOs), and International Governmental Organizations in the reconstruction and development of the Iraqi and Afghan health systems. Army medical personnel have generally sought to do whatever they can to support the complicated and difficult task of rebuilding collapsed or dysfunctional health systems despite a dearth of training, expertise, or doctrine on the subject to guide them. Though the Army Medical Department has over the years maintained to some extent training and doctrine focused on humanitarian assistance and disaster relief missions, there has been no similar attempt to develop and maintain doctrine and training on a far bigger, more complicated, and more protracted mission—health system reconstruction and development during counterinsurgency.

U.S. Army medical personnel have provided aid to civilians in various ways during multiple counterinsurgency campaigns going all the way back to the 19th century.[1] During the prolonged counterinsurgency effort in Vietnam a generation ago, the U.S. Army initiated a large number of programs designed to support the development of the Vietnamese military and civilian health care systems.[2] Unfortunately, in the aftermath of the conflict in Vietnam, there was no institutionalization via training and doctrine of important lessons learned through years of conflict. Counterinsurgency is an exceedingly messy, complicated and difficult form of warfare and once a particular conflict is concluded, the Army, including the Army Medical Department, tends to transition quickly back to focusing on preparation for conventional large-scale operations, and the knowledge gained over years of counterinsurgency gets lost in the process. As a consequence, Army medical personnel end up repeating the same mistakes in different conflicts resulting in the unnecessary loss of life and the waste of large sums of money. It is essential that this process not be repeated as the current counterinsurgency campaign winds down. Instead, the hard-fought lessons learned on the battlefield must be captured and institutionalized in doctrine and training for the benefit of the next generation of Army medical personnel, as the current conflicts will surely not be the last time that the U.S. engages in counterinsurgency.

U.S. military and civilian organizations involved in Afghan and Iraqi health system reconstruction and development have been criticized for the lack of planning prior to the initiation of conflict, inadequate coordination among involved agencies, and poor strategic planning for comprehensive development. U.S. Army efforts in particular have

been criticized for being ad hoc, focused primarily on short-term and high impact

projects, and unconnected with host nation ministries of health.[3] As a result, some

civilian development theorists have recommended a severely circumscribed role for the

U.S. Army in health system reconstruction and development, limited to providing

security, supporting health programs for the Iraqi and Afghan militaries, and providing

temporary emergency services in insecure areas.[4] Many military authors, on the other

hand, after having spent time on the ground in Iraq or Afghanistan, support a significant

role for the military in health system reconstruction and development during

counterinsurgency but have varying opinions about the best way to accomplish this.[5]

This thesis seeks to determine what role the U.S. Army should play, beyond

providing security, in health system reconstruction and development during

counterinsurgency. Chapter 2 includes a historical overview of the involvement of U.S.

Army medical personnel in previous counterinsurgencies, as well as an examination of

current Army and joint doctrine. The third chapter reviews the critiques of military

involvement in Iraq and Afghanistan from the perspective of civilian development

theorists and humanitarian workers. Chapter 4 provides an in-depth look at health system

reconstruction and development in Iraq from the pre-conflict planning stages through the

withdrawal of U.S. forces. It examines the actions of the various civilian and military

organizations involved in health system reconstruction and development, including the

degree of integration and coordination between various groups. Chapter 5 addresses the

ongoing experience with health system reconstruction and development in Afghanistan.

Finally, chapter 6 summarizes the perspectives and experiences presented throughout the thesis to suggest the role the U.S. Army should play in health system reconstruction and development during a counterinsurgency and the corresponding principles which apply.

Primary Research Question

Should the U.S. Army play a significant role, beyond providing security, in health system reconstruction and development while engaged in counterinsurgency?

Secondary Research Questions

In seeking an answer to the primary research question, several secondary research questions will be addressed:

1. What does U.S. military doctrine say on this issue?

2. What are the primary perspectives concerning the proper role of the military and other U.S. Government agencies in health system reconstruction and development while engaged in counterinsurgency?

3. What lessons can be learned from the experience with health system reconstruction and development in Iraq and Afghanistan?

4. Which strategies and what types of military medical operations have been effective in supporting counterinsurgency principles and which have not?

5. What principles should guide health system reconstruction and development in countries confronting insurgencies?

Assumptions

This paper makes the assumption that the U.S. Army will continue to be involved in counterinsurgency into the near future. It also makes the assumption that lessons learned in Iraq and Afghanistan are relevant to counterinsurgencies in other countries, though each counterinsurgency is different.

Definitions

This paper accepts the World Health Organization definition of a <u>health system</u>: (1) all the activities whose primary purpose is to promote, restore and/or maintain health; (2) the people, institutions and resources, arranged together in accordance with established policies, to improve the health of the population they serve, while responding to people's legitimate expectations and protecting them against the cost of ill-health through a variety of activities whose primary intent is to improve health.[6] There are six building blocks which make up a health system: service delivery; health workforce; leadership and governance; health information system; medical products, vaccines, and technologies; and health system financing.

For the purposes of this study:

<u>Health system reconstruction and development</u> refers to the process of rebuilding aspects of the health system that are damaged or destroyed while simultaneously creating new structures and mechanisms for the effective delivery of health care.

<u>Medical civil-military operations</u> are "health related activities . . . that establish, enhance, maintain and influence relations between the joint or coalition force and host nation, multinational governmental authorities and NGOs, and the civilian populace in order to facilitate military operations, achieve U.S. operational objectives, and positively impact the health sector."[7]

<u>Insurgency</u> is defined as "the organized use of subversion and violence by a group or movement that seeks to overthrow or force change of a governing authority."[8]

Counterinsurgency is defined as the "comprehensive civilian and military efforts taken to defeat an insurgency and to address any core grievances."[9]

Two common measures used in assessment throughout the military are measures of effectiveness and measures of performance. This study uses the joint definitions of these terms:

A measure of effectiveness is a criterion used to assess changes in the operational environment that is directly related to the achievement of an objective or the creation of an effect.[10] Measures of effectiveness have to do with the results or consequences of actions and seek to determine whether the results being achieved are making progress towards the desired end state.

A measure of performance is a criterion for assessing friendly action that is directly related to task accomplishment.[11] Measures of performance seek to determine whether a given task or action was performed as the commander intended.

Scope and Delimitations

This paper will look primarily at U.S. Army experiences in counterinsurgency warfare in Iraq and Afghanistan over the last 10 years. Army and joint doctrine published over that time period will be reviewed. In addition, an attempt will be made to identify examples of instances in which U.S. Army units and personnel successfully contributed to Iraqi or Afghan health system development.

In analyzing the development of the Iraqi and Afghan health systems, the analysis will be limited to three of the World Health Organization's six building blocks of health systems: (1) service delivery; (2) health workforce; and (3) leadership and governance. The three remaining health system building blocks (health information system; medical

6

products, vaccines, and technologies; and health system financing) will not be addressed due to space and time limitations.

Limitations

There is a limited amount of quantitative data on the health systems of Iraq and Afghanistan. The data that does exist often comes from more developed and urbanized areas of these countries and data from rural areas is sometimes lacking. In addition, much of the data cannot be independently verified. Conclusions will be drawn primarily based on analysis of the literature and review of the published experiences of individuals and organizations who have worked in these countries.

Significance of the Study

This paper seeks to contribute to the body of theory underlying counterinsurgency warfare and the Army's role in health system reconstruction and development. It is anticipated that answers to the primary and secondary research questions will have ramifications for Army medical doctrine and policies in the future.

Research Design

This study seeks to answer the primary research question, "Should the U.S. Army play a significant role, beyond providing security, in health system reconstruction and development while engaged in counterinsurgency?" As such, it is an exploratory study which looks at two cases: the campaigns undertaken by the U.S. Army in Iraq and Afghanistan over the last 10 years. The study is primarily a qualitative one, concerned with evaluating the involvement of the U.S. Army and other agencies in health system reconstruction and development in Iraq and Afghanistan and identifying significant lessons learned. A review of military doctrine on these subjects will be undertaken with the goal of assessing its suitability to the situation on the ground in these countries. Although the study is primarily a qualitative one, a review of quantitative data that has been gathered on public health indices in Iraq and Afghanistan will be included in the evaluation of effectiveness.

Written documents will be the foundation for research. Primary sources including after action reports and other assessments from U.S. Army personnel who have been involved with health system development in Iraq and Afghanistan will make up the most important group of evidence. In addition, literature on this subject from non-military sources including scholarly articles, reports, and other assessments will be reviewed.

---

[1]Robert J. Wilensky, *Military Medicine to Win Hearts and Minds: Aid to Civilians in the Vietnam War* (Lubbock, TX: Texas Tech University Press, 2004), 18.

[2]Ibid., 48-77.

[3]See, for example, Frederick M. Burkle, Jr., Bradley A. Woodruff, and Eric K. Noji, "Lessons and Controversies: Planning and Executing Immediate Relief in the Aftermath of the War in Iraq," *Third World Quarterly* 26 (2005): 797-814, http://www.jstor.org/discover/10.2307/3993721?uid=3739672&uid=2129&uid=2134&uid=2&uid=70&uid=4&uid=3739256&sid=56108111593 (accessed 11 February 2012); Shakir Jawad (AL-ainachi) et al., "Post-Conflict Reconstruction in the Health Sector: Host Nation Perspective," in *Transitions: Issues, Challenges and Solutions in International Assistance*, ed. Henry R. Yarger, November 2010, 95-110, http://www.dtic.mil/cgi-bin/GetTRDoc?AD=ADA548963 (accessed 25 April 2012); Leonard S. Rubenstein, "Post Conflict Health Reconstruction: New Foundations for U.S. Policy," United States Institute of Peace Working Paper, September 2009, http://www.usip.org/files/resources/post-conflict_health_reconstruction.pdf (accessed 25 April 2012).

[4]Leonard S. Rubenstein, "Health Initiatives and Counter-Insurgency Strategy in Afghanistan," United States Institute of Peace Brief, 5 March 2010, http://www.usip.org/files/resources/PB%2012%20Health%20Initiatives%20and%20Counterinsurgency%20Strategy%20in%20Afghanistan.pdf (accessed 29 April 2011), 4.

[5]See, for example, Jay B. Baker, "Medical Diplomacy in Full-Spectrum Operations," *Military Review* (September-October 2007): 67-73; Edward Lee Bryan, "Medical Engagement: Beyond the MEDCAP" (Monograph, School of Advanced Military Studies, U.S. Army Command and General Staff College, 2008), http://www.dtic.mil/cgi-bin/GetTRDoc?AD=ADA485508 (accessed 5 May 2012); Bret T. Ackermann, "Assisting Host Nations in Developing Health Systems" (Strategy Research Project, U.S. Army War College, 2010), http://www.dtic.mil/cgi-bin/GetTRDoc?AD=ADA522017 (accessed 5 May 2012).

[6]World Health Organization (WHO), *Everybody's Business: Strengthening Health Systems to Improve Health Outcomes* (Geneva, Switzerland: WHO Press, 2007), http://www.who.int/healthsystems/strategy/everybodys_business.pdf (accessed 5 May 2012), 2.

[7]Chairman, Joint Chiefs of Staff, Joint Publication (JP) 4-02, *Health Service Support* (Washington, DC: Government Printing Office, 31 October 2006), IV-7.

[8]Chairman, Joint Chiefs of Staff, Joint Publication (JP) 1-02, *Department of Defense Dictionary of Military and Associated Terms* (Washington DC: Government Printing Office, 2010), 163.

[9]Ibid., 77.

[10]Headquarters, Department of the Army, Field Manual (FM) 3-07, *Stability Operations* (Washington, DC: Government Printing Office, October 2008), Glossary.

[11]Ibid.

CHAPTER 2

HISTORICAL OVERVIEW AND REVIEW OF DOCTRINE

That we have had to spend several years relearning these lessons is a measure of the U.S. defense establishment's failure to take counterinsurgency seriously after the American retreat from Vietnam.

— James Dobbins
New U.S. Commander to Change Iraq Focus

Army medical personnel have been involved with providing aid to host nation civilians while engaged in counterinsurgency throughout multiple conflicts going back to the 19th century. This chapter provides a brief historical overview of U.S. Army experiences with health system reconstruction and development in previous conflicts up to and including the Vietnam War. It also includes an examination of current Army and joint doctrine on the subject of health system reconstruction and development during counterinsurgency.

Historical Overview

Because the vast majority of books and articles concerning the history of the U.S. Army focus on large-scale wars involving conventional operations, many people are not aware that the U.S. Army going back to its origin has actually spent far more years engaged in "small wars," the majority of which have been counterinsurgencies, than in conventional combat operations.[1] U.S. Army medical personnel in each case have been there first and foremost to treat wounded American troops, but in many cases have also provided aid to host nation civilians and in some cases have worked on the reconstruction of host nation health systems. Two significant examples which provide several important

10

historical lessons relevant to today's counterinsurgencies are the Philippines Insurrection and the Vietnam War.

During the U.S. Army's involvement in the Philippines Insurrection that followed the Spanish-American War of 1898, U.S. Army medical personnel played an important role in the Army's pacification strategy directed towards the Filipino countryside. U.S. Army physicians worked side-by-side with Filipino physicians and nurses on multiple campaigns focused on public health, including extensive vaccination programs and measures to ensure a safe water supply.[2] These programs were successful in reducing the country's death rate by 50 percent within the first year.[3] Senior U.S. Army leaders at the time asserted that this statistical data establishing effectiveness was evidence that the Army's public health work was an important element of the pacification strategy because it helped to deprive the insurgency of popular support.[4] Four aspects concerning the involvement of U.S. Army medical personnel in the Philippines Insurrection are important to note and relevant to contemporary health system reconstruction and development during counterinsurgency: (1) the focus was on public health measures which benefited the population as a whole; (2) there was a unity of effort between U.S. and host nation medical personnel; (3) the efforts of U.S. Army medical personnel contributed significantly to the overall success of the war effort; and (4) data was collected which demonstrated the effectiveness of the public health interventions.

Throughout the course of the Vietnam War, U.S. Army medical personnel designed and implemented a number of medical programs to aid Vietnamese civilians. Some were more successful than others, but the most well known is certainly the Medical Civic Action Program (MEDCAP). There were actually two versions of MEDCAP instituted during the Vietnam War: MEDCAP I and MEDCAP II.[5] MEDCAP I, instituted

in 1962, was designed to "establish and maintain a continuing spirit of mutual respect and

cooperation between the Republic of Vietnam Armed Forces and the civilian

population."[6] Under this program, Vietnamese military medical personnel accompanied

by U.S. Army medical personnel provided medical support and preventive medicine to

Vietnamese villagers in remote areas. In 1967, the program became the full responsibility

of the Army, Republic of Vietnam (ARVN).[7] By featuring a unity of effort between

American and Vietnamese military medical personnel and an eventual transition to

complete Vietnamese control, MEDCAP I was implemented in line with the lessons

learned during the Philippines Insurrection. Additionally, by connecting the local

population with host nation military medical forces, MEDCAP I conformed to

counterinsurgency principles.

MEDCAP II, on the other hand, generally ignored previous lessons learned and

counterinsurgency principles. This program is what is normally meant when the term

MEDCAP is used today. Created in 1965 during the surge of U.S. forces into Vietnam,

MEDCAP II involved the direct delivery of medical care to Vietnamese civilians by

uniformed U.S. military medical personnel.[8] MEDCAP II included no involvement of

Vietnamese military medical personnel or Vietnamese government officials and there

was no effort to build support among the population for the Vietnamese military or

government. Instead, the program was designed to gain the cooperation of the local

population, particularly in areas where large numbers of U.S. troops were stationed. Most

of the medical treatment provided by U.S. military medical personnel involved a one day

trip to a remote village during which Army physicians and medics performed cursory examinations of Vietnamese villagers and passed out basic medications.[9] The program

was medically unsound because there was no attempt to do more extensive analysis such

as laboratory or x-ray exams when indicated and there was no follow-up.

Despite the fact that this tailgate medicine program was medically substandard

and ignored basic counterinsurgency principles, it survived the war and became the

popular conception of a MEDCAP. The mistaken notion that these types of MEDCAPs

were a useful tool in a counterinsurgency to "win the hearts and minds" of the local

populace via direct patient care by uniformed American military personnel also survived

the war. MEDCAPs were then adopted by both Army medical personnel and maneuver

unit commanders as the U.S. Army's primary medical engagement strategy. Thirty years

after the American withdrawal from Vietnam, MEDCAPs featured prominently in the

initial phases of the Iraq and Afghanistan conflicts. MEDCAPs failed as a

counterinsurgency tactic during the Vietnam War and in subsequent counterinsurgency

settings because they were medically unsound, lacked coordination with host nation

health officials, neglected training of host nation medical personnel, and did not address

important public health issues.

MEDCAP is not a doctrinal term and has been used to refer to various types of

medical operations. The most common usage refers to single day events involving

tailgate medicine as in Vietnam. The fact that MEDCAPs have no role as a long-term

population engagement strategy in counterinsurgency does not mean that there are not

some occasions when MEDCAPs may be appropriate. In the immediate aftermath of

major combat operations, during humanitarian assistance missions, and in disaster relief

settings, short-term MEDCAPs may well be effective and appropriate. Additionally, larger-scale operations which provide advanced surgical treatments such as cleft palate repair can also be effective. In these settings, Army medical personnel should seek to include host nation medical officials, address key public health issues, and provide training whenever possible.

It is impossible to say just how successful MEDCAPs and other U.S. Army medical operations focused on aid to Vietnamese civilians were in contributing to the achievement of U.S. operational objectives in the war. Unlike in the Philippines Insurrection, there was no attempt to obtain data establishing effectiveness in Vietnam. Data was obtained on performance, such as numbers of patients seen, but this information was incidental to whether or not desired effects were achieved. In his book *Military Medicine to Win Hearts and Minds: Aid to Civilians in the Vietnam War*, Dr. Robert Wilensky concludes that the entire American medical assistance effort "made little impact on the outcome of the conflict" because it did not build support for the Vietnamese government.[10] Wilensky concluded that in future conflicts the emphasis should be on developing capability and training indigenous personnel while U.S. personnel remain as invisible as possible.

Unfortunately, the Army Medical Department did not undertake any type of comprehensive analysis in the immediate aftermath of the Vietnam War concerning whether MEDCAPs and other medical programs were medically sound or contributed to overall success in the war. In the absence of such analysis and understanding, the idea that MEDCAPs were an effective tool for achieving counterinsurgency objectives took root.

Army Medical Department Doctrine

Army medical personnel, like all Soldiers, use doctrine as a guide to action in training and combat. The remainder of this chapter will review current Army and joint doctrine concerning health system reconstruction and development in foreign countries where the U.S. military is involved in counterinsurgency. Overall, Army Medical Department doctrine is extremely limited in its discussion of health system reconstruction and development while engaged in counterinsurgency.

The newly published Army Tactics, Techniques, and Procedures 4-02, *Army Health System*, issued after a decade of war in Iraq and Afghanistan, contains less than one page on support to stability operations.[11] The word "counterinsurgency" does not appear in this publication. Readers are referred to Field Manual (FM) 8-42, *Combat Health Support in Stability Operations and Support Operations,* for additional details. The most recent edition of FM 8-42 is from 1997.[12] The only portions relevant to health system reconstruction and development in FM 8-42 are three pages each on nation assistance and medical support for counterinsurgency.[13] Included are some common sense general precepts for working together with host nation personnel to make assessments, allocate resources, and develop training programs. Army medical personnel are instructed to make assessments of the host nation's military medical infrastructure and capabilities as well as those of the civilian sector. There are no specific details concerning what exactly is involved in working together with host nation personnel to reconstruct a country's health system while the country battles an insurgency. This is the full extent of material on the subject of health system reconstruction and development found in Army Medical Department doctrinal manuals. For the last decade of war, Army

15

medical personnel in Iraq and Afghanistan have been forced to look elsewhere for guidance on this subject.

Other Army Doctrinal Manuals

Beginning with the publication of FM 3-24, *Counterinsurgency,* in 2006, a number of Army doctrinal manuals concerned with counterinsurgency and stability operations have addressed in various ways some of the issues involved with health systems reconstruction and development. The publication of FM 3-24, followed by FM 3-07, *Stability Operations,* and FM 3-24.2, *Tactics in Counterinsurgency*, was a direct reaction to the U.S. military's initial lack of success in its wars in Iraq and Afghanistan. FM 3-24 provides a method for defeating an insurgency via the development of effective governance by a legitimate host nation government, supported by coalition military and civilian personnel.[14] There are actually relatively few references specifically to medicine and health in FM 3-24; however, the method provided for how to conduct counterinsurgency is applicable in some ways to health system reconstruction and development.

FM 3-24 lists essential services as one of the possible logical lines of operation in counterinsurgency. Also mentioned as possibilities are combat operations-civil security operations, host nation security forces, governance, and economic development.[15] The medical treatment and public health of the host nation population are key aspects of these essential services, all of which address the life support needs of the population. Ensuring that the populace has access to these essential services, including medical treatment, is an essential aspect of successful counterinsurgency.

Counterinsurgencies involve a whole host of civilian organizations, both governmental and non-governmental, working alongside military forces. Regarding this, FM 3-24 states:

> In counterinsurgency it is always preferred for civilians to perform civilian tasks. There are many U.S. agencies and civilian IGOs with more expertise in meeting the fundamental needs of a population under assault than military forces have; however, the ability of such agencies to deploy to foreign countries in sustainable numbers and with ready access to necessary resources is usually limited. The more violent the environment, the more difficult it is for civilians to operate effectively. Hence, the preferred or ideal division of labor is frequently unattainable. The more violent the insurgency, the more unrealistic is this preferred division of labor.[16]

In unstable environments, military forces often possess the only available capability to provide essential services to the populace. When civilians are unable to provide these services for whatever reason, military forces are obligated by doctrine to do so.

In addition, FM 3-24 provides a number of principles for successful counterinsurgency. These include the notion that the better learning organizations usually are victorious and that long-term success is founded on assisting people to take control of their own affairs and consent to the government's rule.[17] In addition, unity of effort of the different agencies involved must be present at every level in order to achieve success. Interagency planning teams are essential. The establishment of security for the populace is the cornerstone of all counterinsurgency operations. Without security, the restoration of essential services and the development of effective governance are impossible. The manual also advises Army personnel to develop genuine partnerships with host nation authorities and to employ local leadership and labor as much as possible.

Finally, FM 3-24 explains the clear–hold–build approach to counterinsurgency operations in areas with significant insurgent operations. The initial goal is to create a secure environment by clearing the area of insurgents. Then security forces continue to hold the area while support is built and the population is protected. Throughout the clear–hold–build process, the focus is on providing security for the population, eliminating the presence of insurgents, enforcing the rule of law, and rebuilding local institutions.[18]

FM 3-07, *Stability Operations*, published in 2008, emphasizes the "whole of government" approach to reconstruction and development throughout all sectors, integrating the "collaborative efforts of departments and agencies of the United States government to achieve unity of effort toward a shared goal."[19] FM 3-07 also stresses the importance of building institutional capacity within the host nation as a key to success in stability operations. Building capacity involves creating an environment which promotes community participation, strengthening managerial systems, and developing sustainable training.[20]

The final Army manual which has some relevance for health system reconstruction and development is FM 3-24.2, *Tactics in Counterinsurgency*, published in 2009.[21] FM 3-24.2 goes into greater detail on the importance of support for public health programs. Initial efforts immediately after the cessation of combat operations should involve stabilizing the public health situation within the operational area.[22] This will likely involve assessments of infrastructure, medical logistics, training, and public health programs. It is important to coordinate from the beginning with other actors and agencies working in public health. Other important tasks include assessment of water sources, sanitation, repairing civilian clinics and hospitals, and vaccination campaigns.

Joint Doctrinal Publications

At the outset of the wars in Iraq and Afghanistan, joint doctrinal manuals had little to say about counterinsurgency, and even less about health system reconstruction and development during counterinsurgency. This began to change late in 2005 with the publication of the Department of Defense (DOD) *Instruction on Stability Operations*, which was later updated in 2009. This instruction established "stability operations as a core U.S. military mission that the Department of Defense shall be prepared to conduct with proficiency equivalent to combat operations."[23] In 2006, with the publication of Joint Publication (JP) 4-02, *Health Service Support*, there was for the first time a U.S. military medical manual which devoted significant attention to health system reconstruction and development.[24] The changes to this manual grew directly out of the recent experiences of military medical personnel in attempting to work together with host nation officials to rebuild health systems in Iraq and Afghanistan after the conclusion of major combat operations.

According to JP 4-02, medical civil-military operations are generally performed in coordination with other U.S. government or multinational agencies. The focus of Health Service Support initiatives during medical civil-military operations should be to improve the capacity of host nation officials to provide public health and medical services to the population, leading to increased legitimacy on the part of the host nation government. Joint Force Surgeons are instructed to coordinate closely with civil affairs units and information operations teams to ensure unity of effort.[25] In addition, coordination with other U.S. government civilian agencies, coalition partners, host nation agencies, NGOs, and International Governmental Organizations is deemed essential for successful medical civil-military operations. All projects should be sustainable and the host nation should ultimately have ownership of all of them. In addition, these missions should include cultural awareness training and should enhance the legitimate authority of the host nation government. The Health Service Support staff should include an international health officer or subject matter expert with regional medical expertise and the ability to speak the local language, in order to enhance partnerships with other agencies and the host nation. Health service support representatives should also participate in all available civilian and military coordination mechanisms.

Finally, according to JP 4-02, the provision of Health Service Support and health education via medical civil-military operations can provide a noncontroversial and cost-effective way to support U.S. interests in another country. This may include assisting with the development of the host nation medical infrastructure, developing host nation civilian medical programs, improving basic health and sanitation services, and monitoring civil health indicators.[26]

In 2010, DOD Instruction 6000.16 was published and asserted that:

Medical Stability Operations are a core U.S. military mission that the Department of Defense Military Health System shall be prepared to conduct throughout all phases of conflict and across the range of military operations, including in combat and noncombat environments. Medical Stability Operations shall be given a priority comparable to combat operations and integrated across all Military Health System activities including doctrine, organization, training, (and) education.[27]

The Instruction goes on to say that the Military Health System will develop health sector capacity and capability for indigenous populations when indigenous, foreign, or U.S. civilian personnel are unable to do so. In so doing, military medical personnel should be prepared to work closely with their interagency counterparts, international organizations, NGOs, and private sector individuals. The Assistant Secretary of Defense for Health

Affairs is tasked to implement a Medical Stability Operations education and training program while the secretaries of the military departments are tasked to develop Medical Stability Operations capabilities by organizing and training medical personnel to effectively execute them. Finally, Geographic Combatant Commanders are tasked to incorporate Medical Stability Operations into campaign plans, theater security cooperation plans, training, and planning.[28]

The most recently published joint doctrinal manual which considers health system reconstruction and development is JP 3-07, *Stability Operations*, from September 2011.[29] This manual reflects a decade of war in Iraq and Afghanistan and includes numerous lessons learned during the conduct of stability operations in those two countries. The Department of State (DOS) is given overall responsibility for leading a whole of government approach to stabilization. The primary contribution of the military to stability operations is to protect and defend the population. There are three categories of missions in stability operations: initial response activities, transformational activities, and activities which foster sustainability. Initial response activities involve immediate humanitarian assistance; transformational activities aim to increase security and involve reconstruction; and activities that foster sustainability involve long-term efforts at capacity building.[30]

JP 3-07 defines stability operations as the "build" in the counterinsurgency process of clear–hold–build. The foundation of stability efforts involves strengthening the perception of legitimacy of the host nation government by the population. The restoration of essential services, including public health, is considered a key to achieving security in fragile areas. In addition, human security is a requirement for building and sustaining stability. The human security needs of the population are met when both their personal

21

security needs and their basic physiological needs (e.g., food, water, and shelter) are adequately addressed. The U.S. Agency for International Development (USAID) generally takes the lead in the restoration of essential services. The military should be focused on enabling access to the population for USAID and other civilian organizations where possible; however, only military forces may be able to operate in some insecure areas.[31]

The Development of Doctrine in Response to Wartime Experiences

Military medical personnel in Iraq and Afghanistan in the first several years after the conclusion of major combat operations were confronted with host nation health systems which had been largely destroyed or in some areas had never existed. Unfortunately, there was almost a complete doctrinal void on the subject of host nation health system reconstruction and development. Beginning in late 2005, Army and joint doctrine began to reflect some of the lessons learned from fighting two different counterinsurgencies. FM 3-24, *Counterinsurgency*, laid out the principles of counterinsurgency operations, including the primacy of securing the population, the importance of developing the legitimacy of the host nation government, unity of effort, interagency cooperation, and the restoration of essential services. Various joint publications issued over the next several years, including JP 4-02, *Health Service Support*, discussed the importance of capacity building, sustainability, and host nation ownership when working to develop health systems. However, Army Medical Department doctrinal manuals have thus far continued to lack any significant discussion or analysis on the subject of health system reconstruction and development. In addition, none of the doctrinal publications from the Army or the joint realm go much beyond some basic precepts and principles to lay out concrete details concerning how exactly

organizations go about the process of reconstructing a host nation's health system while

engaged in counterinsurgency.

The next chapter will examine how humanitarian workers and development

theorists view this military doctrine, as well as their perspectives on the experiences of

military personnel on the ground doing health system reconstruction and development.

---

[1]Headquarters, Department of the Army, Field Manual 3-07, *Stability Operations* (Washington, DC: Government Printing Office, October 2008), 1-1.

[2]Wilensky, *Military Medicine to Win Hearts and Minds: Aid to Civilians in the Vietnam War*, 19.

[3]John Morgan Gates, *Schoolbooks and Krags, the United States Army in the Phillipines, 1898-1902* (Westport CT: Greenwood Press, 1973), 134-136.

[4]Robert F. Malsby III, "Into Which End does the Thermometer Go? Application of Military Medicine in Counterinsurgency: Does Direct Patient Care by American Service Members Work?" (Master's Thesis, U.S. Army Command and General Staff College, 2008), http://www.dtic.mil/cgi-bin/GetTRDoc?AD=ADA501911 (accessed 5 May 2012), 37.

[5]Wilensky, *Military Medicine to Win Hearts and Minds: Aid to Civilians in the Vietnam War*, 53-61.

[6]Ibid., 53.

[7]Ibid., 54.

[8]Ibid., 57.

[9]Ibid., 85.

[10]Ibid., 132.

[11]Headquarters, Department of the Army, Army Tactics, Techniques, and Procedures (ATTP) 4-02, *Army Health System* (Washington, DC: Government Printing Office, October 2011), 5-7.

[12]Headquarters, Department of the Army, Field Manual (FM) 8-42, *Combat Health Support in Stability Operations and Support Operations* (Washington, DC: Government Printing Office, October 1997).

[13]Ibid., 3-7-10 and 3-20-23.

[14]Headquarters, Department of the Army, Field Manual 3-24, *Counterinsurgency* (Washington, DC: Government Printing Office, December 2006).

[15]Ibid., 4-5.

[16]Ibid., 2-9.

[17]Ibid., I-21-26.

[18]Ibid., 5-18-21.

[19]Headquarters, Department of the Army, Field Manual 3-07, *Stability Operations*, 1-4.

[20]Ibid., I-35-39.

[21]Department of the Army, Field Manual 3-24.2, *Tactics in Counterinsurgency* (Washington, DC: Government Printing Office, April 2009).

[22]Ibid., 3-12-13.

[23]Department of Defense, Instruction (DoDI) 3000.05, *Stability Operations* (Washington DC: Government Printing Office, 2009), 2.

[24]Chairman, Joint Chiefs of Staff, Joint Publication (JP) 4-02, *Health Service Support.*

[25]Ibid., IV-8.

[26]Ibid.

[27]Department of Defense, Instruction (DoDI) 6000.16, *Military Health Support for Stability Operations* (Washington DC: Government Printing Office, 2010), 1.

[28]Ibid., 1-6.

[29]Chairman, Joint Chiefs of Staff, Joint Publication (JP) 3-07, *Stability Operations* (Washington DC: Government Printing Office, 2011).

[30]Ibid., I-3-4.

[31]Ibid., xxi-xxvii.

CHAPTER 3

CRITIQUES OF MILITARY INVOLVEMENT IN HEALTH SYSTEM

RECONSTRUCTION AND DEVELOPMENT

> Social and economic factors such as basic education, elementary health care, and secure employment are important not only on their own, but also for the role they play in giving people the opportunity to approach the world with courage and freedom.
>
> — Amartya Sen
> *Development as Freedom*

Military medical personnel involved in health system reconstruction and development in Iraq and Afghanistan frequently have worked alongside humanitarian workers from a wide variety of NGOs and international organizations. In general, military personnel and humanitarian workers share a common interest in building the legitimacy and capacity of the host nation government within the health sector. However, there is at times an underlying tension between military strategies focused on counterinsurgency principles on the one hand and humanitarian strategies focused on the promotion of equity and the eradication of poverty on the other. This chapter reviews criticisms of the military's role in health system reconstruction and development from the perspective of theorists and humanitarian workers engaged in development.

Principles of Health System Reconstruction and Development

Critiques of the U.S. military's involvement in health system reconstruction by development theorists are based upon experiences not only in Iraq and Afghanistan but throughout the developing world over the last several decades. Based upon their experiences in helping to build health systems throughout the developing world, in conflict zones as well as in countries relatively free of conflict, development theorists have formulated what has been termed an "emerging international consensus on what principles should guide health system reconstruction and development."[1] Six of these principles are encountered consistently throughout the literature and are particularly relevant to this thesis. The first of these principles is that health system reconstruction and development should take a comprehensive systems-based approach which integrates all six building blocks of a health system: service delivery; health workforce; leadership and governance; health information system; medical products, vaccines and technologies; and health system financing.[2] Because health systems as a whole cannot be strengthened by separating out their different components, isolated actions directed towards short-term goals may temporarily improve one aspect of a country's health system, while weakening the overall system. Planners need to consider the effects their actions will have on the entire health system and seek to develop strategies which are integrated across all six building blocks of health care systems.

Second, health system reconstruction and development should be focused around public health interventions and primary care medicine. In this type of approach, public health measures aimed at ensuring clean water, good sanitation, and methods of disease prevention that benefit the masses of a country are prioritized over more expensive, specialized interventions. In addition, the primary, or first contact, level of a patient with the health care system acts as a foundation for the entire health care delivery system.[3] The principle of providing as much care as possible at the lowest level, backed up by secondary facilities which focus on specialized care, is central to this approach. Continuity of care for the individual patient with his or her primary care provider over

26

time and across levels of care is also essential to this approach. Finally, a focus on maternal and child health is an important component of an approach centered on primary health care.

The third principle is that health system reconstruction and development should strive to create an equitable health system which minimizes systemic disparities.[4] In most health care systems, those who are poor and those who live in rural or remote areas tend to have less access to coverage and receive fewer services. Health system reconstruction and development should seek to correct this pattern as much as possible.

Fourth, there should be an effort to enhance the development of capacity at all levels, from individuals all the way up the Ministry of Health (MOH).[5] Building the institutional capacity of organizations from the smallest level to the highest to lead, plan, and oversee their own health care system is essential to this process.

The fifth principle of health system reconstruction and development is that it should be community-centered. Community members need to be active partners in every step of the development process and should see themselves as co-owners of all programs.[6] In general, priority should be given to community-based clinics in small towns and rural areas over initial large resource commitments to hospitals in wealthier urban areas.[7]

The sixth and final principle is that it is essential to transition as soon as possible from the provision of emergency health services towards building the capacity of the host nation health ministry to implement plans for developing a functional health system.[8] In the immediate post-conflict period, there is an inevitable tension between the need to provide acute health care to people in need and the long-term necessity to build capacity and develop systems which are sustainable. It is important for organizations involved in health system reconstruction and development in post-conflict settings not to get so involved with attempting to meet the acute health care needs of the population that attention to longer term capacity-building projects is completely ignored. Much of the critique of military involvement in health system reconstruction and development from development theorists is centered on their belief that military organizations do not adhere to these principles which have developed out of years of experience with health system reconstruction and development throughout the developing world.

Critique Of the Military's Role In Health System
Reconstruction and Development

Within the development community, there is a diversity of opinion concerning what constitutes the proper working relationship between humanitarian organizations on the one hand and military forces on the other. This chapter outlines the perspectives of some development theorists and humanitarian workers who are generally critical of military involvement in health system reconstruction and development. However, this perspective is not monolithic within the development community. Among NGOs, there is a diversity of viewpoints and practices when it comes to working with military forces during counterinsurgencies. Some, such as Doctors Without Borders and the International Red Cross, value their independence highly and generally have no relationships whatsoever with foreign governmental organizations or military forces.[9] Others, such as World Vision and CARE, have limited contact with foreign governments and militaries but are very careful to distinguish themselves from governmental organizations in their interactions with the local population.[10] A final group, including International Medical

Corps and many faith-based NGOs, cooperates freely with foreign governments and military forces.[11]

In addition, some civilian development experts who have worked with coalition forces in Iraq and Afghanistan have written positively of the military's role in reconstruction and development. Andy Tamas is a development worker who was assigned to a Strategic Advisory Team with Canadian forces in Afghanistan from 2005 to 2006. His book on the subject, *Warriors and Nation Builders: Development and the Military in Afghanistan*, praises the team's work in building support for the Afghan National Development Strategy, coordinating donors, and focusing on the development of capacity.[12]

On the other hand, a number of development theorists are critical of military involvement in health system reconstruction and development. One common criticism, provided by development theorist Carol Messineo, is that "the U.S. military lacks the expertise to address the structural sources of underdevelopment, alienation, and instability in fragile states."[13] According to this view, the reconstruction of a developing country's health system is far too complex and difficult a task for military forces to accomplish. In addition, according to this perspective, military forces base their development strategies on security, political, and tactical objectives. Development workers, on the other hand, make decisions according to what will best promote equity and the eradication of poverty. The fact that military forces are focused on tactical and security objectives rather than development as an end in itself distorts the military's practice of development assistance, according to Messineo.[14] As a result, military support for host nation health system reconstruction and development fails to conform to the six principles outlined earlier in the chapter, according to this development perspective.

Leonard Rubenstein, another development theorist critical of military involvement, asserts that the military prioritizes work in insecure areas or in regions where allegiance to the government is at risk.[15] Development principles, on the other hand, base the deployment of resources on the promotion of equity with a focus solely on where need is greatest. Rubenstein also criticizes military interventions during counterinsurgency for their focus on short-term tactical gains rather than the long-term, capacity-building strategy favored by development principles.[16] According to Rubenstein, counterinsurgency principles and Provincial Reconstruction Team (PRT) guidelines emphasize the importance of achieving immediate results. This short-term focus may be inconsistent with and actually undermine long-term development. Rubenstein argues that the requirements of military strategy and the nature of short-term military deployments make it impossible for the military to link short-term interventions with long-term development objectives.[17]

Some development theorists are critical of FM 3-24, the Army's manual on counterinsurgency, for what they say is a lack of concrete guidance on how to go about actually doing health system reconstruction and other types of development.[18] The manual's failure to include any kind of analytical assessment tool is also criticized. According to Messineo, "the manual expects field commanders to achieve ambitious development goals based upon no more than a chapter's worth of very general guidance, often in environments where active war fighting is occurring in parallel.[19]

Development theorists go on to criticize the military for designing and implementing projects such as the construction of new clinics without prior consultation with the host nation health ministry.[20] According to this view, the military tends to act independently because it has its own funding mechanisms. Messineo asserts that the huge expenditures by military forces in Iraq and Afghanistan working in health system reconstruction and development have "been complicit in the culture of corruption that exists . . . undermining the legitimacy of institutions of state and commerce."[21]

The conclusion of these development theorists is that the military should largely stay out of host nation reconstruction and development.[22] Rubenstein recommends a severely circumscribed role for the military, limited to logistical aid, support for military programs, the establishment of security, and the provision of temporary services in highly insecure areas.[23] Echoing other development theorists, Rubenstein concludes that the resources for health reconstruction now found within the DOD should be transferred to civilian agencies and those agencies should be more robustly funded and staffed.[24]

Critique of Militarized Aid

In 2010, eight NGOs working in Afghanistan published a paper, "Quick Impact, Quick Collapse: The Dangers of Militarized Aid in Afghanistan," on what they saw as the harmful effects of an increasingly militarized aid strategy in the country.[25] Like the development theorists in the previous section, they are quite critical of what they believe is the military's overemphasis on achieving a quick impact with short-term projects rather than on the long-term development of capacity and sustainability. Their paper alleges that military projects are often "poorly executed, inappropriate and do not have sufficient community involvement to make them sustainable."[26] They also state that there is little evidence that the military approach is generating stability. The authors assert that military-dominated institutions, including PRTs, lack the capacity to effectively manage development and are unable to achieve the trust of local communities.[27]

The NGO authors are also critical of what they believe is the inappropriate focus of the militarized aid approach. They quote from the 2009 version of "Commander's Guide to Money as a Weapon," which defines aid as a "non-lethal weapon" to be used to win the hearts and minds of the indigenous population and to facilitate defeating the insurgents.[28] The authors go on to list a multitude of projects overseen by the military and PRTs in Afghanistan which they describe as short-term, feel-good projects which failed to consider larger strategic and capacity-building implications. These include poorly designed schools which were never used due to shoddy construction and the lack of adequate consultation with the local community. They are also critical of U.S. funding mechanisms, including the Commander's Emergency Response Program (CERP), which prohibits funds from being used for project maintenance or upkeep.[29] Finally, the authors are critical of the lack of monitoring of the impact of military and PRT projects and the lack of oversight.

The NGO authors go on to say that while military and PRT projects have in some cases helped address immediate needs, they have more importantly delayed the process of rebuilding Afghan institutions.[30] They attempt to make the case that coalition militaries and PRTs are weakening the accountability of the Afghan government to its people by assuming responsibilities that the Afghan government should be filling. Like the development theorists, they believe that the military does have a role to play in providing assistance in insecure areas where civilian actors are unable to do so, but they think that this aid should be provided impartially and on the basis of need rather than according to military tactical goals or counterinsurgency principles.[31] The authors are furthermore critical of the military for focusing development on insecure areas in the southern and eastern regions of Afghanistan while neglecting stable, but desperately poor, regions in the North and West. Like the development theorists, they believe that all health system reconstruction in Afghanistan, including that overseen by the military, should be based solely upon what will yield the best outcome for Afghans, rather than on political or military objectives. They conclude with a recommendation to gradually phase out militarized forms of aid to enable military institutions to return to a focus on security, while at the same time increasing the funding of national and international civilian organizations to take the place of the military in Afghan health system reconstruction and development. They also recommend a greater role for the United Nations (UN) in delivering and coordinating aid.[32]

Critique of Comprehensive Approaches

"Civil-Military Relations: No Room for Humanitarianism in Comprehensive Approaches" is an article by Stephen Cornish and Marit Glad from CARE, an international humanitarian organization devoted to fighting global poverty, focused particularly on the needs of women.[33] The authors are critical of what they term a "comprehensive" approach to stabilization and reconstruction in which military, political, and development efforts are complimentary instruments.[34] They believe that aid has become increasingly politicized and militarized since 11 September 2001, and that since then "the security agenda has largely trumped the human security agenda to the detriment of vulnerable populations and of the development and humanitarian actors which come to their assistance."[35] Like the development theorists and the NGO authors, Cornish and Glad are critical of what they see as the use of development and humanitarian assistance by the military as a strategy to win hearts and minds and appease communities, instead of being based exclusively on the criteria of need and aid effectiveness.[36]

Cornish and Glad are most concerned about the impact that the militarization of aid has had on NGO security. They write that since the end of the Cold War there has been an evolution from neutral humanitarian assistance to what they call "forcible humanitarian interventions," which are founded upon political and strategic considerations rather than on need alone.[37] In their view, the U.S. military views humanitarians as potential force multipliers in these new conflicts and has sought ways to coordinate and control their actions in order to obtain the maximum of strategic benefit. This results in the subordination of humanitarian and development aid programming to political interests in ways that are counterproductive, according to the authors.

Cornish and Glad go on to say that there has been a significant increase in violence against humanitarian workers since the development of the "comprehensive" approach to aid.[38] They do concede that "there seems to be no clear correlation between attacks on NGOs and the intensity of the conflict or the presence of specific military actors," but are nevertheless deeply concerned about the overall increase in attacks of a political nature on aid workers throughout the world.[39] International data does show that the "number of attacks in which aid workers were killed, kidnapped, or injured has risen significantly since 1997" with a particularly sharp increase from 2006 to 2008.[40] The reasons for this increase are multifactorial, with commentators disagreeing on primary causes.[41] Cornish and Glad are particularly concerned about the role of PRTs in blurring the distinction between the military and aid workers since, according to the authors, PRTs seek primarily to achieve the political ends of their sponsoring governments by working to improve security and governance in conflict regions. Like many other humanitarian workers, they are concerned about what they believe is the "loss of humanitarian space" which occurs as a result of military involvement in aid and development. Humanitarians abide by the core principles of humanity, independence, and impartiality, which are codified in UN General Assembly Resolution 46/182.[42] The authors believe that military activities in the humanitarian space jeopardize the perceived neutrality of aid workers, endangering them and reducing the operating space for civilian organizations.

According to the authors, NGOs are generally unable to operate in insecure areas, limiting their ability to access populations in need. Aid organizations have had to largely withdraw from the eastern and southern regions of Afghanistan due to these security constraints. The recommendation of the authors for their fellow humanitarian workers is to attempt to maintain independence in programming and to keep a clear distance from military actors.[43]

The Development Perspective

The development perspective on the proper role of the military in health system reconstruction and development, as outlined in this chapter, is encountered throughout the literature on humanitarian aid and development, though there are countercurrents which are more supportive of military involvement. According to this perspective, there is a fundamental conflict and tension between development strategies on the one hand and military, or counterinsurgency, strategies on the other. Development theorists believe that health system reconstruction and development should be based on the principles of humanity, independence, and impartiality with equity and the eradication of poverty as primary goals. Because military activities are frequently based, instead, on other tactical or political goals, by definition these activities result in unsuccessful or inappropriate forms of reconstruction and development, according to many development theorists and humanitarian workers.

In addition, according to development theorists, military forces lack the skills required to effectively assist development. Military actors, according to this view, are inevitably focused on short-term interventions at the expense of the development of sustainability and capacity over the long-term. Military medical personnel are furthermore unable to establish a proper working relationship with host nation health ministry officials because military actors will ultimately act in accordance with their own funding mechanisms and objectives, rather than those of the host nation health ministry.[44] The result, according to development theorists, is a "loss of humanitarian space" as aid becomes increasingly militarized and politicized, putting humanitarian workers increasingly at risk and unable to operate in insecure areas.

The next chapter will examine how health system reconstruction and development has played out in Iraq with particular attention to the role of the military and bearing in mind the criticisms of development theorists outlined in this chapter.

---

[1]Rubenstein, "Post-Conflict Health Reconstruction: New Foundations for U.S. Policy," 19.

[2]Robert C. Swanson et al., "Toward a consensus on guiding principles for health systems strengthening," *PLoS Med* 7, no. 12 (December, 2010), http://www.plos medicine.org/article/ info:doi/10.1371/journal.pmed.1000385 (accessed 29 April 2012).

[3]World Health Organization, *Everybody's Business: Strengthening Health Systems to Improve Health Outcomes*, 15.

[4]Swanson et al., "Toward a consensus on guiding principles for health systems strengthening."

[5]Ibid.

[6]Health and Fragile States Network, "Health Systems Strengthening in Fragile Contexts: A Report on Good Practices and New Approaches," June 2009, http://www.bsf-south-sudan.org/sites/default/files/Good_Practice_Report_final.pdf (accessed 29 April 2012), 50.

[7]Rubenstein, "Post-Conflict Health Reconstruction: New Foundations for U.S. Policy," 19.

[8]Ibid., 3.

[9]Ellen B. Laipson, "Information-Sharing in Conflict Zones: Can the USG and the NGOs Do More?" *Studies in Intelligence* 49, no. 4 (2005): 55-64, https://www.cia.gov/library/center-for-the-study-of-intelligence/csi-publications/csi-studies/studies/vol49no4/USG_NGOs_5.htm (accessed 3 May 2012).

[10]Ibid.

[11]Ibid.

[12]Andy Tamas, *Warriors and Nation Builders: Development and the Military in Afghanistan* (Kingston, Ontario: Canadian Defense Academy Press, 2009).

[13]Carol Messineo, "The United States Military as an Agent of Development: Counterinsurgency Doctrine and Development Assistance," International Affairs Working Paper 2010-05, October 2010, http://www.gpia.info/files/u706/Messineo_2010-05.pdf (accessed 3 May 2012), 3.

[14]Ibid.

[15]Rubenstein, "Health Initiatives and Counter-Insurgency Strategy in Afghanistan," 4.

[16]Rubenstein, "Post-Conflict Health Reconstruction: New Foundations for U.S. Policy," 33.

[17]Ibid.

[18]Carol Messineo, "The United States Military as an Agent of Development: Counterinsurgency Doctrine and Development Assistance," 11-12.

[19]Ibid., 12.

[20]Rubenstein, "Post-Conflict Health Reconstruction: New Foundations for U.S. Policy," 34.

[21]Carol Messineo, "The United States Military as an Agent of Development: Counterinsurgency Doctrine and Development Assistance," 13.

[22]Ibid., 17.

[23]Rubenstein, "Post-Conflict Health Reconstruction: New Foundations for U.S. Policy," 10.

[24]Ibid.

[25]Ashley Jackson, *Quick Impact, Quick Collapse: The Dangers of Militarized Aid in Afghanistan*, January 2010, http://www.scribd.com/doc/25889897/Oxfam-Quick-Impact-Quick-Collapse (accessed 29 April 2012).

[26]Ibid., 1.

[27]Ibid., 2.

[28]Ibid., 1.

[29]Ibid., 2.

[30]Ibid.

[31]Ibid.

[32]Ibid., 5.

[33]Stephen Cornish and Marit Glad, "Civil-military Relations: No Room for Humanitarianism in Comprehensive Approaches," *Security Policy Library*, 5-2008, http://reliefweb.int/node/24781 (accessed 5 May 2012).

[34]Ibid., 3.

[35]Ibid.

[36]Ibid.

[37]Ibid., 4.

[38]Ibid., 5.

[39]Ibid., 6.

[40]Abby Stoddard, Adele Harmer, and Victoria DiDomenico, "Providing aid in insecure environments: 2009 Update," Humanitarian Policy Group Policy Brief 34, April 2009, http://www.odi.org.uk/resources/docs/4243.pdf (accessed 1 May 2012), 2.

[41]Ibid., 5-10.

[42]United Nations, "United Nations General Assembly Resolution 46/182," 19 December 1991, http://ochaonline.un.org/cap2006/webpage.asp?Page=1951 (accessed 29 April 2012).

[43]Cornish and Glad, "Civil-military Relations: No Room for Humanitarianism in Comprehensive Approaches," 18-21.

[44]Rubenstein, "Post-Conflict Health Reconstruction: New Foundations for U.S. Policy," 34.

CHAPTER 4

THE IRAQ EXPERIENCE

> History will judge the war against Iraq not by the brilliance of its military
> execution, but by the effectiveness of the post-hostilities activities.
> — Lieutenant General Jay Garner
> *Hard Lessons: The Iraq Reconstruction Experience*

For many years, Iraq's health care system was considered one of the best in the entire Middle East and patients from neighboring countries frequently traveled to Iraq in pursuit of high quality health care. This began to change as the system suffered during Iraq's involvement in a series of conflicts beginning with the Iran-Iraq War in the 1980s. By the time of the U.S.-led military intervention in 2003, the Iraqi health care system was in dire straits. This chapter examines the reconstruction and development of the Iraqi health care system, with particular attention to the role of the military.

The Iraqi Health Care System Prior to the 2003 Invasion

In the mid-1980s, Iraq had one of the most developed and effective health care systems in the Arab world. The system provided primary and specialized health care to 97 percent of the population in urban areas and 79 percent of the population in rural areas.[1] During the 1970s and the first few years of the 1980s, Iraq experienced significant improvements in the majority of its health indicators including significantly reduced infant and under-five mortality rates.[2]

The health care system in Iraq traditionally was organized much like the British health care system. It was oriented around high-technology hospitals and required the large-scale supply of medicines, equipment, and personnel.[3] Prior to Iraq's entry into a succession of conflicts beginning with the Iran-Iraq War in 1980, this capital-intensive system worked fairly well for a significant percentage of the Iraqi populace as a result of the relative strength of Iraq's economy.[4] The system also had three important weaknesses which were to play a key role in the reconstruction process beginning in 2003: the lack of a public health focus, the absence of a formal mechanism to collect data on health indicators, and the lack of a strategy for effectively developing human resources.[5]

Iraq's health care system has for many years included extensive public as well as private delivery systems.[6] The Iraqi public health care system includes hundreds of primary health clinics throughout the country, as well as hospitals which provide specialized care at the provincial and district levels. The private health sector in Iraq includes a large number of primary care clinics, small hospitals, and pharmacies throughout the country.[7] Traditionally, Iraqi health care personnel have worked in government facilities in the morning and in private clinics, pharmacies, and hospitals in the afternoon. However, the private health sector has suffered chronically from strict regulations imposed by the government, as well as from a lack of investment.[8] During the periods of economic sanctions, the private health sector was able to supplement some of the services provided by the beleaguered public sector.

The Iraqi health care system began to deteriorate during the 1980s and continued to do so for the next three decades as a result of almost continuous war, exacerbated by a decade of economic sanctions.[9] Spending on health care began to decrease during the latter stages of the Iran-Iraq War as Saddam Hussein focused his spending on the military. The situation only got worse during the 1990s as a result of the 1991 Gulf War and subsequent economic sanctions.[10] Iraq's health care infrastructure was seriously

41

affected by the 1991 Gulf War. During the 1990s, there was a 90 percent decrease in funding for health care and critical health indicators fell sharply as a result.[11] In addition, Iraq was unable to restore damaged buildings or replace necessary medical equipment. A great many health care workers also chose to leave the country as a result of the worsening economic conditions, caused in large part by economic sanctions.

In the latter part of the 1990s, the Iraqi MOH adopted a partial fee-for-service system in an attempt to generate more money after many years of fully subsidizing health care for the population. These mechanisms created a two-tiered system which offered higher-quality health care services for those who could afford to pay and inadequate services for those who could not.[12] These efforts were ultimately unsuccessful in raising more money and led to greater inefficiency and unequal access to health care services throughout the country. In 1996, the UN Security Council established the Oil-For-Food Program, according to which Iraq was allowed to export oil in exchange for food and medical supplies.[13] However, the program was employed primarily for political purposes and had a negligible effect on the ability of Iraq's health care system to meet the needs of the population.[14]

Iraq's health care system continued to decline in the years leading up to the invasion in 2003. Communicable diseases, including cholera, typhoid, dysentery, and hepatitis, continued to increase in incidence throughout the country.[15] In addition, expenditures on public health continued to plummet. The MOH's annual budget decreased from $450 million before 1992 to approximately $22 million in 2002, a 96 percent decrease in spending per capita.[16] At the time of the invasion in March 2003, the national stock of critical medical equipment and supplies was dangerously low.[17] By

March 2003, Iraq's health care system was in crisis. Over three decades of war and economic sanctions had transformed it from one of the best in the region into one completely unable to meet the needs of the Iraqi people.

Pre-Conflict Planning for Relief and Reconstruction

Traditionally, post-conflict relief and reconstruction efforts are overseen by the U.S. State Department. The State Department's Office of Foreign Disaster Assistance and USAID normally deploy an operational on-site Disaster Assistance Response Team (DART). The DART is designed to get on the ground quickly and is involved in initial assessment, development of project proposals, liaison with the military, and funding of international relief organization programs for immediate relief.[18] In planning for post-conflict relief and reconstruction in Iraq, U.S. State Department planners assumed that they might face a humanitarian disaster. Though DARTs typically include fewer than 10 people, the DART for Iraq included 80 people due to the unpredictable potential consequences of the conflict.[19] The vast majority of the DART had previous experience in complex emergencies including refugee care, epidemiology, military liaison, public affairs, security, and biological, chemical and nuclear threat analysis.

However, in January 2003, acting on President Bush's directive, the Pentagon created the Office of Reconstruction and Humanitarian Assistance to oversee relief and reconstruction efforts, including coordination with all U.S. and international organizations.[20] This was highly unusual since responsibility for relief and reconstruction traditionally belongs to the State Department. Instead, the DOD would oversee all relief and reconstruction efforts in Iraq. The Office of Reconstruction and Humanitarian Assistance was to be in charge of all operational and policy requirements with regard to humanitarian relief, reconstruction, and national as well as local governance.[21] As a consequence of President Bush's directive, most of the pre-conflict planning for humanitarian relief was done in secrecy by military authorities, leaving the State Department agencies which normally oversee this kind of planning mainly in the dark.[22] In addition, because the Office of Reconstruction and Humanitarian Assistance was a DOD agency, many UN agencies and NGOs were not willing to coordinate and collaborate with the U.S. due to concerns about remaining independent and impartial.[23] As a result, most of the planning for initial humanitarian relief, as well as initial efforts at reconstruction, involved little or no coordination between the various civilian and military agencies involved. As time went on, this lack of civil–military coordination would come to be a recurring theme.

DOD planners believed that there would be little population displacement or public health infrastructure damage as a result of the conflict.[24] They also assumed that reconstruction could be carried out primarily by the private sector, with funding from oil revenues and support from a cooperative Iraqi population.[25] The organizations which were supposed to provide the majority of the immediate humanitarian relief were U.S. military Civil Affairs units and the DART. However, the extent of public health expertise on Civil Affairs teams is generally very limited.

The trajectory of health system reconstruction and development, from the end of major combat operations in late April 2003 until the departure of U.S. troops in December 2011, can be divided into four periods: (1) The immediate aftermath of major combat operations until the transfer of authority from the Coalition Provisional Authority to the interim Iraqi government (April 2003 to June 2004); (2) Growing insurgency and destabilization (July 2004 to December 2006); (3) The surge in U.S. forces (January 2007 to July 2008); (4) Stabilization and drawdown (August 2008 to December 2011). Each period will be considered separately.

<u>The Immediate Aftermath of Major Combat Operations</u>
<u>(April 2003 to June 2004)</u>

On 19 March 2003, coalition forces moved into Iraq from Kuwait as major combat operations began. By 14 April 2003, major combat operations in and around Baghdad were concluded and on 1 May 2003, President Bush declared that the war was over. The fighting did not create large numbers of Internally Displaced Persons within the country or cause large numbers of refugees to cross the Iraqi borders. Neither was there extensive damage to civilian infrastructure such as highways, bridges, and power stations. However, widespread looting throughout the country and pervasive social disorder resulted in the destruction of numerous public facilities and the disruption of essential public services, including health care. Throughout Iraq, hospitals, clinics, pharmaceutical stores, laboratories, and administrative offices were looted and ransacked, resulting in the virtual collapse of the already fragile Iraqi health care system.[26] In addition, the disruption throughout Iraq of essential services including electricity, water, police, public transportation, and communication systems made it next to impossible for patients to travel to obtain health care and for health workers to do their jobs. Hospital directors cited the lack of security, water, and electricity as their three major concerns in the months immediately after the cessation of major combat operations.[27]

Between May 2003 and June 2004, the Coalition Provisional Authority, headed by U.S. Ambassador L. Paul Bremer III, oversaw all reconstruction activities in Iraq.

During the initial post-conflict period, J. K. Haveman, formerly the director of public health for the state of Michigan, oversaw the Iraqi MOH.[28] In September 2003, he turned the position over to an Iraqi health minister, Khudair Fadhil Abbas. On 28 March 2004, the MOH was officially turned over to the Iraqis and became the first autonomous Iraqi ministry. During the first few months after the end of major combat operations, all military and civilian medical and relief organizations were focused on meeting the many immediate humanitarian needs of the Iraqi people. Though there were no significant epidemics or humanitarian catastrophes, it quickly became apparent to those on the ground that there were a number of significant challenges and obstacles affecting those organizations which were beginning the work of health system reconstruction and development.

Civil-Military Coordination

The failures of coordination and integration among the multitude of military and civilian organizations, which first developed during the planning process leading up to the invasion, expanded during the period immediately following major combat operations. The virtual collapse of the Iraqi health system created a situation in which it was absolutely essential that civilian and military organizations work closely with Iraqi MOH officials to collectively and urgently confront immediate problems. Unfortunately, there was no effective mechanism for these organizations to work together and ultimately there was little coordination or unity of effort.[29] The DOD was in charge of interagency coordination but had no formal way of coordinating with other U.S. government agencies, NGOs, and international organizations. As a result, various organizations carried out unilateral initiatives without the appropriate planning and integration with host nation authorities or with other groups working on health system reconstruction and development, resulting in frequent duplications of effort, waste, and projects that did not reflect the needs or desires of Iraqi government officials or the Iraqi people.

During the initial months after the end of major combat operations, there was a vacuum of leadership over the Iraqi health system as all of the different organizations involved in the initial stages of reconstruction and development sought to identify the major issues and begin the rebuilding process. Unfortunately, during this initial period, both U.S. civilian and military organizations were unsuccessful in forging an effective partnership with the host nation in the planning and implementation of reconstruction projects. Most of the major initial policy decisions, which were so important because they established the initial foundations and structures upon which further efforts would build, were made by U.S. administrators along with a handful of Iraqi exiles with little knowledge of existing processes within the MOH.[30] For instance, the new organizational structure of the MOH was created without significant participation from Iraqi officials. Many Iraqis believed that this multilayered system created too many opportunities for duplication, corruption, and administrative confusion.[31] In addition, little effort was made initially to consult with the World Health Organization and other multilateral institutions which had spent years working with the Iraqi MOH. The de-Baathification policy of the Coalition Provisional Authority also prevented many of the senior MOH officials with significant experience from participating in the reconstruction process.

Because U.S. planners had made the assumption that the stabilization and reconstruction process would be brief, there were no processes or mechanisms in place for identifying and evaluating individuals at both the local and national level for

47

participation in the reconstruction of the health system. Instead, U.S. military and civilian officials frequently made rapid assessments on their own of what they believed was needed and then quickly went about implementing their own proposals. This resulted far too often in the construction of clinics or hospitals which Iraqi officials did not want and as a result were not used at all or not used effectively. Far too often, American efforts during this period were perceived by Iraqi officials and medical practitioners as "foreign, unnecessary, and condescending of existing institutional knowledge, policy, capabilities, and practices."[32]

Initial U.S. Army Efforts

U.S. Army and other coalition military units were also confronted with the collapsed Iraqi health care system and the vacuum in leadership. Following the conclusion of major combat operations, Army medical personnel throughout Iraq sought to develop and implement solutions to aid in the reconstruction of the Iraqi health care system, but they were completely unprepared to do so and had done no planning for this contingency prior to their arrival in Iraq. The experiences of Army medical personnel in the 82nd Airborne Division and the 101st Airborne Division during Operation Iraqi Freedom I are representative.

The 101st Airborne Division was based out of Mosul and led by David Petraeus, then a Major General, during Operation Iraqi Freedom I. According to LTC Michael Place, their division surgeon at the time, his division's medical team was forced to take the lead on all medical civil-military operations in that part of Iraq due to a shortage of other agencies doing health system reconstruction in that part of the country at that time. In addition, there were very few military civil affairs personnel with medical

48

experience.[33] According to Place, there were also very few NGOs and USAID was notably absent in their area of operations at that time. As a result, the military medical community was "intimately involved in the development of the medical portion of the entire reconstruction effort."[34] Throughout their one year deployment, there were no current national plans from the MOH, the corps surgeon, or the civil affairs brigade. As a result, division surgeon's sections were forced to develop their own priorities despite their lack of training and staffing for health system reconstruction and development.

The 82nd Airborne Division operated in Al Anbar province from September 2003 until March 2004. As with the 101st Airborne Division, the 82nd's medical team encountered an Iraqi health system in crisis with an absence of leadership and oversight. The 82nd division surgeon at the time, LTC Frank Christopher, and his team eventually took over command and control of all medical civil-military operations in the area, since no one else was doing so.[35] They did so despite the fact that they had not planned to conduct these types of operations, did not have any personnel with expertise in health system reconstruction, and lacked anyone on their team with formal training in civil affairs, facilities evaluation, pay agent operations, contracting, or the Iraqi culture. The 82nd division surgeon's team received assistance from a company grade nurse officer from the attached civil affairs brigade as well as from the organic G-5 section (civil-military operations) and engineers. The medical personnel from the 82nd worked closely with local medical leaders in the area including the Al Anbar provincial medical director.

Over time, the medical team from the 82nd developed a medical civil-military operations budget of $500,000 per week with over 500 individual projects.[36] Because they were task organized and prepared to provide combat health support only to their own troops, these operations quickly overwhelmed available resources. In addition, there was no available medical civil-military operations doctrine to follow and very few lessons learned from Afghanistan or elsewhere which were applicable. Despite all that, the 82nd medical team over the course of its tour spent over $11.5 million of CERP funds to rehabilitate the infrastructure of the Al Anbar medical system, including providing standardized equipment, furniture and diagnostic sets, training of the Iraqi National Guard in basic medical skills, development of a distribution system for medical supplies, and setting the conditions for hospital construction efforts.[37]

The 82nd Airborne Division's medical civil-military operations team did not have much success in working with civilian organizations and agencies in the Al Anbar province during this time period. Both USAID and the Research Triangle Initiative had representatives working in the 82nd's area of operations. However, neither of these groups was able to execute quickly enough to meet the needs of the maneuver commander.[38] For example, over 115 primary and secondary health clinics in Al Anbar province were physically reconstructed during this time. The Research Triangle Initiative initially planned to accept bids and pay for 10 clinic rehabilitations every two weeks. After 12 weeks, they had accepted bids on seven but had not yet started work on any. During the same time period, the 82nd Airborne Division's team was able to do its own bidding, contracting, and paying on the rehabilitation of over 50 clinics.[39] The 82nd's medical team was also told that the Red Crescent Society and a number of NGOs had conducted large-scale assessments in the area and were planning projects, but none of these projects ever came to fruition. Finally, the government of Japan came into the province with the intention of supporting the reconstruction effort. They met with the

50

82nd's team in an effort to prioritize projects. However, the day after the meeting, several of the Japanese delegates were killed by insurgents and the 82nd's medical team never again heard from the Japanese government. Overall, the poor security situation in the major cities of Al Anbar province, Fallujah and Ramadi, severely constricted the freedom of civilian agencies to participate in the reconstruction of the health system in this area.

For both the 82nd and the 101st, as well as for the medical teams from other Army units operating throughout Iraq at this time, there was little or no guidance from higher civilian or military medical authorities concerning priorities for health system reconstruction and development. As a result, each military medical unit, from the platoon level all the way up to division, was forced to develop and implement its own programs for supporting health system reconstruction and development in its area of operations. The result was a complete lack of synchronization and integration between tactical level efforts throughout Iraq and strategic level planning.

Strategic Planning

In August 2003, the Iraqi MOH began to hold priority setting workshops as part of its strategic planning. Participants included representatives from the MOH, the Coalition Provisional Authority, the UN, NGOs, International Governmental Organizations, and other health system stakeholders.[40] Nine different working groups were established and continued to meet throughout 2003 and 2004, leading to the creation of an Iraqi MOH strategic vision and plan which would eventually be approved by the Iraqi Minister of Health. This strategic vision included five important goals: the provision of high-quality, affordable, accessible health care for all Iraqis; the elimination of corruption; a shift from a hospital-based, curative model of health care to a primary care-

51

based, preventive model; increased autonomy for local health care directors; and a decrease in the infant mortality rate by 50 percent by the end of 2005. The Iraqi MOH also signed a detailed memorandum of agreement with the Ministry of Defense which provided for MOH personnel and logistical support for the Iraqi armed forces.[41] Overall, the strategic vision and plan for the reconstruction and development of the Iraqi health system represented a realistic vision of an attainable end which would serve the interests of the Iraqi people. However, this vision document did not include an implementation plan to guide the MOH in designing and carrying out projects which accomplished the outlined goals.[42]

The Security Situation

Shortly after the end of major combat operations, the security situation across Iraq began to deteriorate. The worsening security situation had a profound impact on the reconstruction and development of the health system. It simultaneously increased the Iraqi people's need for health services while it made efforts to provide these services much more difficult. Asked what he believed were the three most urgent problems for the Iraqi health system two weeks after the end of major combat operations, the World Health Organization representative in Baghdad stated "security, security, and security."[43] This lack of security kept both patients and staff from going to the clinics, out of fear of looters and other dangerous elements.

The bombing of the UN Headquarters in Baghdad on 19 August 2003, for which Al Qaeda claimed responsibility, killed 22 people and wounded more than 100 others. This bombing targeted the UN assistance mission which had been created just five days earlier. A second bombing one month later resulted in the withdrawal of 600 UN staff members from Iraq.[44] Many other NGOs, international organizations, and civilian contractors also left the country. Those who remained, including those working on health system reconstruction and development, had severely restricted mobility and freedom to operate. In most areas of the country, there were few organizations available to do the work necessary to achieve the goals of the Iraqi MOH strategic vision and plan. USAID, which according to U.S. policy should play a key role in health system reconstruction and development, was severely restricted from doing anything in most areas of the country and was most active in Baghdad. In many areas, military units were the only entities able to act and thus they were forced to step in and do what they could to rebuild the Iraqi health system despite their lack of training, expertise, and doctrine.

Growing Insurgency and Destabilization
(July 2004 to December 2006)

In late June 2004, the Coalition Provisional Authority officially transferred sovereignty to the interim Iraqi government. Within the Iraqi MOH, the transition strategy appeared to be focused on transferring resources and leadership for existing projects to Iraqi officials as quickly as possible. Sufficient time was not provided to develop a comprehensive plan for integrating ongoing reconstruction projects into a strategic plan for the health system. In addition, the Iraqi officials chosen to take leadership of the MOH generally lacked the capacity to take ownership of ongoing programs to make them succeed. Iraqi MOH officials in leadership positions at that time lacked the ability to successfully guide health system reconstruction and development via policy development, strong oversight, and personnel management.[45] This failure of the transition process to set the new Iraqi MOH leadership up for success represented the

53

continuation of the largely disjointed, ad hoc, and poorly coordinated coalition effort since the end of major combat operations.

Over the next 2 1/2 years, sectarianism, corruption, and poor governance at the national level would grow throughout Iraq, including within the MOH. In the highly politicized atmosphere which dominated the various Iraqi ministries, Moqtada al-Sadr, a sectarian Shiite leader fundamentally opposed to the U.S., was able to gain control of the MOH and quickly went about replacing skilled technocrats with party loyalists. As al-Sadr gained increasingly more control of the ministry, resistance to U.S. and coalition assistance would grow and complicate the reconstruction effort.

As the insurgency grew and the security situation worsened over the next several years, the Iraqi health system continued to suffer. Perhaps most harmful to the reconstruction effort was the departure of approximately 18,000 Iraqi physicians, about half the national total, who abandoned jobs in government clinics and hospitals and sought refuge abroad.[46] In addition, thousands of nurses discontinued working in government facilities. This departure of key personnel literally crippled the Iraqi health care system. Medical professionals who worked in government facilities became a target of the insurgency and at least 628 physicians were killed according to Iraqi government estimates.[47]

Efforts to Improve Interagency Coordination

Difficulties with U.S. government interagency coordination and integration permeated not only the health system but essentially all aspects of the U.S. stabilization and reconstruction effort in Iraq. In an effort to improve the situation, the Office of the Coordinator for Reconstruction and Stabilization was created within the U.S. State

54

Department to coordinate a "whole of government" federal effort concerning stability and reconstruction operations. In December 2005, President Bush signed National Security Presidential Directive-44, which outlined the responsibilities of the new office. At the same time, the Defense Department issued DOD Directive 3000.05, *Military Support for Stability, Security, Transition, and Reconstruction (SSTR) Operations*, which established stability operations as a core U.S. military mission and called for the development of doctrine, organizations, training, education, exercises, material, leadership, personnel, facilities, and planning in support of this effort.[48] The directive also asserted that integrated civilian and military operations were the key to success in stabilization. It directed that the stability operations dimensions of military planning should be closely integrated with the plans of other U.S. government agencies, relevant multinational organizations, international organizations, NGOs, and private sector groups.

In the Iraqi health sector, there continued to be a "critical need for improved coordination across the Department of Defense, U.S. government, host nation, coalition, international organization, and NGO leadership."[49] In January of 2007, an Iraqi Health Sector Reconstruction After Action Review, which included a diverse cross-section of subject matter experts from the DOD, Coalition Provisional Authority, other U.S. government agencies, NGOs, and Iraqi health officials, recommended the creation of a "medical staffing model" to merge military efforts with interagency and host nation (MOH) representation, such as through a coalition joint interagency task force approach.[50] They recommended that this model include a clear outline of the roles and missions of each of the contributing organizations, top-down training for civil-military interactions, and clear guidance for interagency collaboration, as specified in National

Security Presidential Directive-44 and DOD Directive 3000.05. Unfortunately, such a model of interagency collaboration and integration with host nation officials was not established and difficulties with duplication of effort and the failure of integration would continue.

U.S. Army Projects

In the years between the transfer of sovereignty in June of 2004 and the surge of forces in January 2007, U.S. Army medical personnel in units scattered throughout Iraq largely found themselves on their own when it came to developing and implementing plans for reconstruction and development of the health system. As the insurgency increased in strength throughout many areas of the country and the security situation deteriorated as a result, there were large swathes of the country where there were no civilian organizations working on health system reconstruction and development. There were civilian agencies and multinational organizations working with the MOH in Baghdad but their work had little to no effect on Army medical personnel working in rural or insurgent-laden areas of the country. Instead, each battalion and brigade surgeon throughout the country in conjunction with his own medical team went about interacting with the Iraqi civilian and military health systems in his own way.

The method most familiar to Army company, battalion, and brigade commanders was the MEDCAP, in which Army medical personnel, as discussed in relation to the Vietnam War, provided direct patient care on a short-term basis to local Iraqi villagers. MEDCAPs were considered by many American commanders as a fairly easy way to make positive inroads with the local population, while at the same time providing needed medical care to medically underserved villagers. Given their lack of preparation, planning, training, and doctrine for health system reconstruction and development, it is

perhaps not surprising that Army medical personnel and their commanders initially chose

to employ the MEDCAP as one of their primary tools for the health sector. The problem

with MEDCAPs as a long-term medical engagement strategy in counterinsurgency, as

discussed in chapter 2, is that they are medically unsound because they often provide

substandard acute care without any mechanism for follow-up or continuity of care. In

addition, MEDCAPs did not contribute to the development of capacity or sustainability

within the Iraqi health system nor did they provide for the training of Iraqi medical

personnel. In fact, MEDCAPs undermined the local health care system and thus

decreased the population's support for its own local government. They acted in

opposition to the primary counterinsurgency principle of improving local governance and

connecting the people to their own government.

However, because MEDCAPs were the most well-known tool in the kitbag,

particularly on the part of commanders, they were a common occurrence throughout Iraq

during this period. Too often, medical and combat arms officers alike saw MEDCAPs

and other forms of medical civil-military operations as a "drive-by operation for

supporting pacification, gathering local intelligence, or rewarding locals for their

cooperation."[51] During the first 3 to 4 years after the end of major combat operations, the

principles for how to wage successful counterinsurgency had not yet been inculcated into

the vast majority of U.S. Army personnel on the ground in Iraq (or their leadership) and

so there was frequently little consideration about how various operations affected the

legitimacy of the Iraqi government or the people's confidence in their own government.

Instead, MEDCAPs seemed like a good idea to many Army medical personnel and commanders because they appeared on the surface to be an easy way to build goodwill towards Americans.

Task Force 30th Medical Brigade provided medical support to Multinational Corps–Iraq from late 2005 until early 2007. Their after action review discusses their efforts in the area of medical civil-military operations.[52] Task Force 30th Medical Brigade was involved with the reconstruction and development of both the Iraqi military and civilian health care systems throughout this period. Their focus was on the development of the health system of the Iraqi security forces, and they worked together with the Iraqi Surgeon General to develop systems for medical training, medical logistics, medical operational planning, and physician recruitment.[53] In addition, Task Force 30th Medical Brigade distributed over $40 million worth of class VIII medical supplies to provinces throughout Iraq in support of the Iraqi civilian health system.[54]

During this time period, many coalition military units became involved with the building or reconstruction of hospitals and clinics. Commanders authorized the use of CERP funds for these actions. CERP funds were designed for short-term projects which could immediately assist the local population. More importantly, they were not designed to provide for the development of long-term sustainability and capacity within the health system or other sectors. Unfortunately, too many Army units quickly authorized the building or reconstruction of medical facilities without first consulting with local MOH officials or performing comprehensive assessments of current capacity along with a projection of needs. As a result, millions of dollars were spent on hospitals and clinics which were never completed or never used because no one within the Iraqi MOH would take ownership. Many of these projects did not make sense in terms of local or national health system resources and priorities. The Task Force 30th Medical Brigade after action review gives an example of a battalion which used CERP funds to build a clinic without first notifying local MOH officials or local civil affairs units. Once completed, the local representative from the Iraqi MOH refused to staff the clinic or to supply it.[55] In this case, as in many other similar situations, a short-term photo op turned into a long-term public-relations disaster.

As time went on, the Task Force 30th Medical Brigade civil-military operations team came to realize that the MEDCAPs then occurring throughout Iraq were not only not contributing to health system reconstruction and development, but were in many cases actually hindering these efforts. As a result, they recommended that all MEDCAPs be discontinued and replaced by "Cooperative Medical Engagements." Cooperative Medical Engagements were defined as "specific humanitarian opportunities led by Iraqi civilian or military medical personnel for which American involvement is incidental to the overall engagement."[56] Each Cooperative Medical Engagement was to focus on assisting Iraqi civilian or military health officials to provide for the medical care of their own populations. Eventually, all Cooperative Medical Engagements required the approval of the Multinational Corps–Iraq surgeon and units had to demonstrate that each project would advance Multinational Corps–Iraq security goals, improve access and influence, increase stability, and generate goodwill prior to approval. The replacement of MEDCAPs by Cooperative Medical Engagements over the next several years by units operating throughout Iraq was proof that U.S. Army medical personnel and their commanders were learning some things from their initial mistakes and working to develop operations which contributed to capacity building and improved Iraqi governance, in conjunction with counterinsurgency principles.

Provincial Reconstruction Teams

PRTs are civil-military organizations designed to operate in semi-permissive environments.[57] They were initially deployed as a transitional mechanism to improve security and facilitate reconstruction and economic development.[58] PRTs were designed as a mechanism for extending good governance, security, and economic development beyond the central government in Baghdad to provincial and local officials across Iraq. They were first implemented in Iraq in 2005. PRTs in Iraq were under State Department control and were led by a senior Foreign Service Officer with a military deputy. Each PRT sought to combine military capability with civilian expertise as a way to overcome the difficulties of interagency collaboration. PRTs worked to accelerate the development of civic, economic, and governance capacities in insecure areas.[59] During this time, there were 10 PRTs operating in provincial capitals throughout Iraq. Each team was made up of 30 to 80 members from civilian agencies including the State Department and USAID, as well as military members. However, there were no health care personnel in the original design of the PRTs operating in Iraq and thus they had little or no effect on Iraqi health system reconstruction and development.[60] Beginning in 2007, embedded Provisional Reconstruction Teams (ePRTs) were deployed and included a small number of health care personnel. These teams will be discussed in the next section.

The Surge in U.S. Forces (January 2007 to July 2008)

The surge in U.S. forces that began in January of 2007 corresponded with three important events which opened the doors for significant improvements in the Iraqi health system after years of stagnation. First, in November of 2007, the government of Iraq announced that Dr. Salih M. al-Hasnawi would serve as the next Minister of Health. Dr. Salih is a psychiatrist who was committed to the reform of the Iraqi health care system after several years of stagnation and domination of the MOH by loyalists to al-Sadr. One of Dr. Salih's initial key objectives was the repatriation of Iraqi physicians who had left the country. He established programs under which Iraqi physicians who chose to serve in rural areas could receive free land in return and also substantially increased the salaries paid to Iraqi physicians. These programs were initially quite successful and resulted in the hiring of over 1000 Iraqi physicians by the MOH in their first year.[61] Second, the publication of FM 3-24, *Counterinsurgency,* in 2006, and the subsequent widespread adoption of counterinsurgency tactics by U.S. Army units, including their medical personnel, led the way to the use of more effective techniques for building capacity within the Iraqi health system. Finally, the improvements in security which accompanied the surge of U.S. forces and the political reconciliation with large segments of the Sunni leadership, created the necessary space for civilian organizations throughout the country to work on the reconstruction and development of the Iraqi health system.

U.S. Army Efforts during the Surge

The adoption of counterinsurgency tactics by U.S. Armed Forces in Iraq did not begin on a significant scale until it had become painfully clear that conventional tactics were not working against the growing insurgency in Iraq. The publication of the

Counterinsurgency manual in 2006 helped to build momentum, and the installation of General David Petraeus as Multinational Forces-Iraq Commander in February 2007 established the primacy of the counterinsurgency methodology. The *MNF-I Commander's Guidance*, released early in 2008, distilled the philosophy down into a series of principles, most of which were directly applicable to the reconstruction and development of the Iraqi health system.[62] These included the necessity of securing the population since the people were the decisive terrain; the importance of actually living among the people in their neighborhoods; the need to generate a unity of effort among interagency partners, the host nation, and NGOs; the importance of fostering the legitimacy of the Iraqi government; and the necessity of looking for sustainable solutions.[63]

The Battle for Tal Afar in northwestern Iraq is considered by many to be the first successful counterinsurgency campaign of the war. From the summer of 2005 until the winter of 2006, Colonel H.R. McMaster's 3rd Armored Cavalry Regiment (ACR) successfully implemented the counterinsurgency methodology in order to build the capacity and legitimacy of the local government, secure the population, and restore essential services in the area. Major Jay Baker was the regimental surgeon at the time and led the way in ensuring that medical civil-military operations played a key role in his unit's successful strategy. He wrote an article about his team's efforts which was published the next year in *Military Review* and served as a template for others to follow.[64]

The 3rd ACR's medical team focused on building the capacity and capability of local medical institutions as a way of increasing the legitimacy of the Iraqi government in the minds of the local population. One of the key reasons for the success of the 3rd

ACR's medical team was that its plans consistently corresponded with and were nested in the strategy of the regiment as a whole. By the time of the unit's arrival in the city of Tal Afar, Al Qaeda had infiltrated the city's only hospital and the hospital's director was reportedly sympathetic with the insurgents.[65] The local population was afraid to visit the hospital and outpatient visits had fallen to less than 10 per day. The 3rd ACR began their operation by positioning one of their units in an overwatch position near the hospital, preventing injured insurgents from continuing to receive care there. A few months later, this overwatch mission was passed off to an Iraqi Army unit.

In the fall of 2005, Operation Restoring Rights was successful in restoring security to the city, setting the conditions for subsequent medical civil-military operations.[66] Baker notes in his article that 3rd ACR's higher headquarters had prohibited MEDCAPs but that no alternative policy guidelines or doctrine existed. In addition, there were no civil affairs public health teams available. The 3rd ACR medical team instead organized their own teams, which they called Medical Clinic Action Teams, to interact with local medical institutions.[67] They began by conducting assessments of the administration, clinical operations, and infrastructure of the hospital and then worked together with local officials on numerous projects including ambulance repair, the supply of medicines, and preventive medicine instruction. One of the key benefits of their team's work was that it created the opportunity for increased engagement with the Iraqi medical personnel working in local facilities and ultimately led to the creation of strong relationships between Iraqi and U.S. Army medical personnel. This relationship building, which can come only as a result of sustained, consistent, day-to-day work at the local level, is absolutely essential to the success of any counterinsurgency strategy.

The 3rd ACR medical team would go on to build strong relationships with local NGOs and medical representatives from local Iraqi security forces, in addition to Iraqi physicians and MOH officials. They helped organize a regional medical society with the goal of enabling it to become a self-sustaining professional organization. By February 2006, the hospital was seeing over 800 patients per day and female physicians had returned to work.[68] Adopting the counterinsurgency model as a guide, Baker proposes that the principles of successful medical civil-military operations are "secure, engage, and build."[69] First, the establishment of security for local clinics and hospitals is essential. Second, units should engage consistently with local Iraqi medical leaders in order to understand the needs and wants of the population in their area of operations. Finally units should then build medical capacity within their area.

Embedded Provincial Reconstruction Teams

In January 2007, President Bush announced that the PRT program in Iraq was being expanded with increased PRT staffing throughout the country and the fielding of 10 embedded PRTs in three key areas: around Baghdad and in Anbar and Babil provinces.[70] Embedded PRTs were smaller and leaner versions of the traditional PRTs. Whereas the focus of traditional PRTs was at the provincial level, the ePRT mission was to support military counterinsurgency efforts at the district and local levels by improving governance, fostering economic development, and improving essential public services including health.[71] Each ePRT was embedded in an Army Brigade Combat Team or Marine Corps Regimental Combat Team and was led by a State Department Foreign Service Officer. Each team also included representatives from the military, USAID, interpreters, and other government agencies such as the U.S. Department of Agriculture.

Unlike traditional PRTs, the ePRTs included medical representation which varied from team to team but frequently included personnel from the U.S. Public Health Service-Centers for Disease Control and Prevention. The State Department initially was unable to fill the majority of the ePRT positions and as a result most of the slots had to be filled by military personnel.[72]

In their efforts to improve governance, foster legitimacy, and restore essential services including the reconstruction and development of the Iraqi health system, ePRTs faced many of the same challenges previously discussed in reference to Army units. First, as with Army medical personnel, "the vast majority of medical personnel assigned to ePRTs had little experience in health policy, health planning, or the management of health care systems within international or interagency systems."[73] And they received little relevant training on reconstruction and development of health systems prior to deployment. In addition, some ePRT members complained about the lack of any sense of operational direction because they had not received any strategic guidance from the embassy in Baghdad or from any other higher authority. As a result, they were never able to adequately determine whether their efforts were making progress towards achieving some strategic end state and led to a somewhat haphazard approach to reconstruction.

The same lack of unity of effort that had confounded relationships between U.S. military and civilian organizations since the pre-conflict planning phase continued to be an issue for the ePRTs. There were multiple chains of command: through the military, the Office of Provincial Affairs, the Embassies, and representatives of the departments and agencies based in Washington D.C.[74] The ePRTs lacked clear lines of authority and, as with most other interagency structures in Iraq, coordination procedures between civilian

65

and military organizations were generally disjointed or nonexistent. Some ePRTs were directed primarily by the Brigade Combat Team Commander while others were led mainly by the State Department Foreign Service Officer. Because the ePRTs and their embedded Brigade Combat Teams each had their own separate agendas, it was not uncommon for representatives from each to meet with the same Iraqi official around the same time period, without any coordination between the two groups.

The difference in time orientation between Army units and many civilians on the ePRTs continued to be an issue, with the Army generally focused on short-term gains while the ePRTs, particularly their USAID representatives, tended to work on multiyear projects aimed at building capacity. Army units, including their medical personnel, often moved into a decimated area and quickly initiated a wide variety of reconstruction projects including clinics and hospitals. This was frequently problematic because it occurred without consultation with the Iraqi MOH and because "just funding projects for the Iraqi government replaced capacity rather than developing it."[75] Even as late as 2008, the Army continued to focus on these kinds of rapid infrastructure development projects using CERP funds, rather than on the concept of developing sustainability. This practice of doing projects for the Iraqi government, rather than finding ways to enable them to do things for themselves, retarded the development of capacity within the Iraqi health system rather than developing it.[76]

Finally, ePRTs, like conventional PRTs and Army units working on health system reconstruction and development, were unable to say how well they were doing because they had no metrics for determining this.[77] There was some good performance data collected, such as number of clinics built and number of patients seen, but there were no good metrics developed to measure the effectiveness of various interventions. This failure goes back to the lack of strategic guidance and agreed upon objectives. Neither the DOD nor the DOS adopted an "ends, ways, and means" approach to measuring the progress of PRTs or their advancement toward operational and strategic goals.[78] Army units were notorious for measuring their performance primarily in terms of what percentage of their CERP funds were spent during a given period, though obviously this had no certain relationship to the achievement of effects.

Stabilization and Drawdown (August 2008 to December 2011)

As a result of the positive effects of the surge in U.S. forces, the effective adoption of counterinsurgency tactics, and political reconciliation with the Sons of Iraq, there was a gradual and sustained improvement in the security situation throughout Iraq. This allowed civilian organizations to begin work on the Iraqi health system in areas where they had previously been unable to do so. On 30 June 2009, U.S. combat forces officially withdrew from the cities and towns of Iraq and returned to their forward operating bases.

The Iraqi MOH under the direction of Dr. Salih continued to make improvements in the Iraqi health system with support from their partners including coalition forces, USAID, various NGOs and multinational organizations. In the "International Compact with Iraq," Dr. Salih spelled out the MOH's objectives and priorities.[79] He established as policy the idea that public health and primary care principles would guide the future development of the Iraqi health system. The World Health Organization officially returned to Iraq in July 2008, five years after they had withdrawn following the bombing of the UN Headquarters in Baghdad, and began to provide policy guidance and various other forms of support to the Iraqi MOH. The Iraqi MOH would remain in the lead for all future operations as the U.S. took on a supportive role as technical advisors.

Military Efforts

Despite the drawdown in U.S. forces, some Army medical units continued to play a role in the reconstruction and development of the Iraqi health system, particularly the health system of the Iraqi security forces. Many of these units were able to capture some of the lessons learned over the previous several years in order to more effectively support health system reconstruction and development. The 21st Combat Support Hospital (CSH) is an example of a unit that was successful in employing some of the newer medical civil-military operational techniques during this time period.[80] The 21st CSH deployed to Al Asad Airbase in western Iraq in January 2010 and was located adjacent to the Iraqi 7th Army Division Headquarters. They were directed to advise and assist the Iraqi 7th Army medical personnel in improving the quality of care provided to 7th Army troops in their clinic.[81] Their self-imposed constraints included using only existing Iraqi clinic infrastructure (as opposed to replacing it), avoiding the employment of unsustainable means (items that could not be continued beyond the departure of the 21st CSH), no spending of money, and no transfer of supplies to the Iraqi Army.[82] They identified as their terminal goal an Iraqi clinic staff able to successfully conduct patient assessments, provide basic treatment based upon protocols, utilize a pharmacy, and successfully operate a medical supply system.

Direct bedside teaching of the Iraqi Army medical personnel by U.S. Army medical staff on a consistent basis served as the foundation of the mission. The Iraqi Army medics had received training in the past but this was the first time they had undergone a sustained practical application. Over time, the Iraqi Army medical personnel grew significantly in their ability to diagnose and treat patients. There were also significant improvements in the organization and utilization of the pharmacy and medical supply system. Despite not spending any money, transferring any supplies, or using unsustainable means, the 21st CSH succeeded in their small "advise and assist" mission to help develop the health system of the Iraqi security forces. The 21st CSH physicians wrote that "in contrast to big-ticket investments in construction, formal education, and long-term advising, our modest effort yielded fairly large returns, at least locally."[83] The 21st CSH managed to avoid the temptation to provide the "quick fixes" which had doomed other U.S. Army units such as providing Iraqis with supplies or pharmaceuticals, rebuilding their clinics, or treating their patients. All of these apparent solutions would have been unsustainable and would have created continued dependence on U.S. support, rather than the development of capacity. The 21st CSH personnel, like so many other U.S. Army units which were effective in health system reconstruction and development, found that the building of relationships with the Iraqi Army personnel through daily shoulder to shoulder interaction was fundamental to their success.

One final issue which came up during this time period involved support provided by U.S. forces to the Iraqi military's health care system. Because the Iraqi military health system competed for the same resources as the civilian health system, overseen by the MOH, there was a perception by many that those in the Iraqi military were getting the better of the severely limited resources. The leadership of the Iraqi military health system and the civilian MOH leaders were able to come together on this issue and ultimately the Iraqi Surgeon General accepted the need to place development of the military medical system as a lower priority, agreeing to open military health care facilities to civilians as well.[84] The issue for the U.S. military and other organizations concerned how much time and money should be devoted to reconstruction and development of the Iraqi military health system, versus the reconstruction and development of the Iraqi civilian health system. The U.S. Army during most of the time it was in Iraq had medical personnel involved in both, though the greater number of personnel and money seemed to be devoted to development of the military health system at the expense of the civilian health system. The problem was that reconstruction of the two health systems was completely stovepiped, so that those working on one had no connection to the other. In addition, there was no systematic attempt at analysis to determine where emphasis should be directed at any given time in order to maximize opportunities to enhance local government and defeat the enemy.

Overview of Iraqi Health System Reconstruction and Development

Widespread insurgency significantly complicated the reconstruction and development of the Iraqi health system. Many of the errors and missteps which would come to characterize the approach of the U.S. government as a whole were first in evidence during the planning process prior to major combat operations, during which there was little to no coordination and integration between military and civilian agencies. This failure on the part of different agencies of the U.S. government to work together to rebuild the Iraqi health system in a whole of government approach would continue throughout the course of U.S. involvement in Iraq and was one of the primary reasons for the many difficulties. The end of major combat operations revealed a collapsed Iraqi health system which had been decimated by decades of war. Over the next several years, as the insurgency grew in strength and the security situation deteriorated, it was not safe for civilian organizations to operate in most parts of Iraq. As a result, the U.S. Army in many cases became the primary agent responsible for the reconstruction and development of the health system. Army medical personnel confronted this situation with little or no expertise in health system reconstruction and development, inadequate resources, no prior training, and no relevant doctrine. At the same time, thousands of Iraqi physicians and other medical personnel departed the country out of fear. Despite all this, some U.S. Army units developed innovative solutions to do what they could in support of health system reconstruction and development.

Unfortunately, U.S. Army units working in the health sector too often focused initially on short-term projects including infrastructure development, without adequate consultation with host nation authorities or adequate assessment. In addition, there was too often an emphasis on short-term security gains, rather than capacity building and sustainability. The fact that the Iraqi MOH was led by al-Sadr and his followers for several of these years only compounded the problem. The surge in U.S. forces which began in January 2007 and the adoption of counterinsurgency tactics by the medical personnel from some U.S. Army units resulted in better local outcomes. However, this good work done by some Army units at the tactical level was generally not tied to strategic efforts at the national level. In addition, the Army, PRTs, and other organizations working on health system reconstruction and development never developed effective metrics for assessing the effectiveness of their interventions at the local or the national level.

Stuart Bowen, the U.S. Special Inspector General for Iraqi Reconstruction,

summed up many of the failures that plagued U.S. government efforts in the

reconstruction and development of the Iraqi health system in a devastating critique in

2010:

> I think that the single largest failed program has been the health sector. The plan
> was to build a state-of-the-art children's oncology hospital in Basra, to construct
> 151 public health care clinics, taking a new level of aid out to the hinterlands in
> Iraq and to refurbish the many broken-down hospitals across the country. None of
> those programs really succeeded.[85]

Audits conducted by Bowen's team of the nearly $1 billion poured into the Iraqi health

sector by the U.S. government documented large cost overruns, delays, poor planning and

waste.[86] This includes nearly $150 million spent on advanced medical equipment which

sat idle because Iraqi doctors were not trained to use it. Bowen concluded that "the health

sector was the worst" and was the sector that fell the furthest short of expectations.[87]

The most recent data from the World Health Organization on health indices for

the Iraqi health system paints more of a mixed picture. Overall, the system has yet to

recover from decades of war but has made progress in some areas, particularly over the

last several years as the security situation has improved. On the positive side, between

2000 and 2010, there were small improvements in several key indicators, including the

infant mortality rate, which declined from 34 deaths per 1000 live births to 31; the under-

five mortality rate, which declined from 43 deaths per 1000 live births to 39; and the

maternal mortality rate, which declined from 84 deaths per 100,000 live births to 75.[88]

On the other hand, despite the return of some Iraqi medical personnel from abroad over

the last several years, at 6.9 physicians for every 10,000 people, Iraq remains far below

the regional average of 11.0.[89] Life expectancy at birth declined from 68 years in 2000 to

66 years in 2010.[90] Child immunization rates have decreased nearly 20 percent since 2000 and the rates of tuberculosis are orders of magnitude higher than in neighboring countries Syria and Jordan.[91]

A retrospective analysis of the entire course of Iraqi health system reconstruction and development in light of the six principles discussed in chapter 3 which should serve to guide the process reveals a mixed picture. On the positive side, over time U.S. Army medical personnel and PRTs did come to focus on the development of capacity and, more often than not, sought to ensure that local initiatives remained community-centered. On the negative side, there was an initial failure to quickly transition from emergency relief to health system reconstruction and a comprehensive systems-based approach was not taken. In addition, there was too frequently a focus on specialized care and advanced medical equipment, rather than on public health and primary health care.

Table 1 demonstrates the progress over time within the three health system building blocks which are the focus of this thesis: health service delivery, the health workforce, and leadership-governance of the health system. With the exception of the Diphtheria, Tetanus, and Pertussis (DTP3) immunizations for one year olds, which showed a slight decrease, the other indicators within all three building blocks demonstrated slow but steady progress toward health system strengthening.

The next chapter will examine the reconstruction and development of the Afghan health system over the last decade during a period of growing insurgency, including a look at some of the similarities and differences with the experience in Iraq.

[1]Center for Economic and Social Rights, "The Human Costs of War in Iraq," 2003, http://www.cesr.org/downloads/Human%20Costs%20of%20War%20in% 20Iraq.pdf (accessed 29 April 2012).

[2]World Health Organization, Eastern Mediterranean Regional Office (EMRO), "Health Systems Profile: Iraq," 2005, http://www.emro.who.int/iraq/pdf/ HealthSystemsProfile.pdf (accessed 29 April 2012), 8.

[3]Jawad et al., "Post-Conflict Reconstruction in the Health Sector: Host Nation Perspective," 99.

[4]Ibid.

[5]Ibid.

[6]Ibid.

[7]World Health Organization, "Health Systems Profile: Iraq," 15.

[8]Jawad et al., "Post-Conflict Reconstruction in the Health Sector: Host Nation Perspective," 100.

[9]Phyllis Bennis, Martha Honey, and Stephen Zunes, "The Failure of U.S. Policy toward Iraq and Proposed Alternatives," *Foreign Policy in Focus* (1 June 2001). http://www.fpif.org/articles/the_failure_of_us_policy_toward_iraq_and_proposed_alterna tives (accessed 29 April 2012).

[10]Jawad et al., "Post-Conflict Reconstruction in the Health Sector: Host Nation Perspective," 100.

[11]Ibid.

[12]Seth G. Jones et al., *Securing Health: Lessons from Nation-Building Missions* (Santa Monica, CA: RAND Corporation, Center for Domestic and International Health Security, 2006), http://www.rand.org/pubs/monographs/2006/RAND_MG321.pdf (accessed 29 April 2012), 225.

[13]Ibid., 223.

[14]Jawad et al., "Post-Conflict Reconstruction in the Health Sector: Host Nation Perspective," 100.

[15]Jones et al., *Securing Health: Lessons from Nation-Building Missions*, 228.

[16]Ibid., 225.

[17]Jawad et al., "Post-Conflict Reconstruction in the Health Sector: Host Nation Perspective," 100.

[18]Burkle, Woodruff and Noji, "Lessons and Controversies: Planning and Executing Immediate Relief in the Aftermath of the War in Iraq," 2.

[19]Ibid.

[20]Jones et al., *Securing Health: Lessons from Nation-Building Missions*, 271.

[21]Burkle, Woodruff, and Noji, "Lessons and Controversies: Planning and Executing Immediate Relief in the Aftermath of the War in Iraq," 3.

[22]Ibid.

[23]Jones et al., *Securing Health: Lessons from Nation-Building Missions*, 271.

[24]Burkle, Woodruff, and Noji, "Lessons and Controversies: Planning and Executing Immediate Relief in the Aftermath of the War in Iraq," 3.

[25]Ibid.

[26]Ibid., 4.

[27]Ibid.

[28]Jones et al., *Securing Health: Lessons from Nation-Building Missions*, 246.

[29]Scott Feil, "Building Better Foundations: Security in Postconflict Reconstruction," *Washington Quarterly* 25, no. 4 (Autumn 2002): 97-109.

[30]Jawad et al., "Post-Conflict Reconstruction in the Health Sector: Host Nation Perspective," 103.

[31]Ibid., 104.

[32]Ibid., 105.

[33]U.S. Army Medical Department Lessons Learned, "Discussion on Civil-Military Operations: Division Surgeons Community of Practice," (October-December 2004), http://lessonslearned.amedd.army.mil/ (accessed 11 February 2012).

[34]Ibid.

[35]Ibid.

[36]Ibid.

[37]Ibid.

[38]Ibid.

[39]Ibid.

[40]David A. Tarantino, Jr. and Shakir Jawad, "Iraq Health Sector Reconstruction: An After-Action Review," Uniformed Services University of the Health Sciences, 9-11 January 2007, http://csis.org/images/stories/globalhealth/ Iraq%20AAR%20final% 201%20OCT.pdf (accessed 29 April 2012), 25.

[41]Ibid., 27.

[42]Jawad et al., "Post-Conflict Reconstruction in the Health Sector: Host Nation Perspective," 106.

[43]Jones et al., *Securing Health: Lessons from Nation-Building Missions,* 258.

[44]Kim Ghattas, "Mixed Feelings over UN Iraq Role," *BBC News*, 11 August 2007.

[45]Jawad et al., "Post-Conflict Reconstruction in the Health Sector: Host Nation Perspective," 106.

[46]Paul C. Webster, "Iraq's health system yet to heal from ravages of war," *The Lancet* 378, no. 9794 (September 2011): 864.

[47]Ibid.

[48]Department of Defense, Instruction (DoDI) 3000.05, *Stability Operations.*

[49]Tarantino, and Jawad, "Iraq Health Sector Reconstruction: An After-Action Review," 8.

[50]Ibid., 5.

[51]Baker, "Medical Diplomacy in Full-Spectrum Operations," 69.

[52]Headquarters, 30th Medical Brigade, "Operation Iraqi Freedom 05-07 After Action Review," http://lessonslearned.amedd.army.mil (accessed 11 February 2012).

[53]Ibid., 25.

[54]Ibid.

[55]Ibid., 110.

[56]Ibid.

[57]Center for Army Lessons Learned, *PRT Playbook,* No. 07-34, September 2007, 1.

[58]Nina Abbaszadeh et al., "Provincial Reconstruction Teams: Lessons and Recommendations," Princeton University Woodrow Wilson School of Public and International Affairs, January 2008, http://wws.princeton.edu/research/pwreports_f07/wws591b.pdf (accessed 29 April 2012), 5.

[59]Ibid., 47.

[60]Thomas S. Bundt, "Synchronizing U.S. Government Efforts toward Collaborative Healthcare Policymaking in Iraq" (Strategic Studies Institute, U.S. Army War College, March 2010), http://www.strategicstudiesinstitute.army.mil/pubs/display.cfm?pubid=978 (accessed 29 April 2012), 5.

[61]Bruno Himmler, "Health Care Diplomacy: The Iraq Experience and How It Can Shape the Future," *Military Medicine* (December 2009), xviii.

[62]David Petraeus, "Multinational Force–Iraq Commander's Counterinsurgency Guidance," *Military Review* (September-October 2008), http://usacac.army.mil/CAC2/MilitaryReview/Archives/English/MilitaryReview_20081031_art004.pdf (accessed 6 May 2012), 2-4.

[63]Ibid.

[64]Baker, "Medical Diplomacy in Full-Spectrum Operations."

[65]Ibid., 70.

[66]Ibid.

[67]Ibid.

[68]Ibid., 72.

[69]Ibid., 73.

[70]John K. Naland, "Lessons from Embedded Provincial Reconstruction Teams in Iraq," United States Institute of Peace Special Report, October 2011, http://www.usip.org/files/resources/SR290.pdf (accessed 1 May 201), 2.

[71]Ibid.

[72]Ibid., 3.

[73]Bundt, "Synchronizing U.S. Government Efforts toward Collaborative Healthcare Policymaking in Iraq," 5.

[74]U.S. House of Representatives Committee on Armed Services, Subcommittee on Oversight and Investigations, "Agency Stovepipes versus Strategic Agility: Lessons We Need to Learn from Provincial Reconstruction Teams in Iraq and Afghanistan," April 2008, http://democrats.armedservices.house.gov/index.cfm/files/serve?File_id=20ca518e-0183-433f-be5a-7e872dbc41b7 (accessed 1 May 2012), 22.

[75]Blake Stone, "Blind Ambition: Lessons Learned and Not Learned in an Embedded PRT," *Prism* 1, no. 4 (September 2010): 147-158. http://www.ndu.edu/press/lib/images/prism1-4/Prism_147-158_Stone.pdf (accessed 29 April 2012), 154.

[76]Ibid.

[77]U.S. House of Representatives Committee on Armed Services, Subcommittee on Oversight and Investigations, "Agency Stovepipes vs. Strategic Agility: Lessons We Need to Learn from Provincial Reconstruction Teams in Iraq and Afghanistan," 28.

[78]Ibid.

[79]Himmler, "Health Care Diplomacy: The Iraq Experience and How It Can Shape the Future," xix.

[80]David C. Lynn and Robert A. De Lorenzo, "Advising and Assisting an Iraqi Army Medical Clinic: Observations of a U.S. Military Support Mission," *Military Medicine* 176 (September 2011): 998-1002.

[81]Ibid., 998.

[82]Ibid., 999.

[83]Ibid., 1001.

[84]Himmler, "Health Care Diplomacy: The Iraq Experience and How It Can Shape the Future," xx.

[85]National Public Radio, "Following the reconstruction money in Iraq," 30 August 2010, http://www.npr.org/templates/story/story.php?storyId=129535004 (accessed 1 May 2012).

[86]Stephanie McCrummen, "Man-made emergency at Iraq's hospitals," *Washington Post*, 10 May 2011.

[87]Ibid.

[88]World Health Organization, "Global Health Observatory Repository, Countries, Iraq," http://apps.who.int/ghodata/?vid=10700&theme=country (accessed 5 May 2012).

[89]Ibid.

[90]Ibid.

[91]Webster, "Iraq's health system yet to heal from ravages of war," 3.

CHAPTER 5

THE AFGHANISTAN EXPERIENCE

During a time of continued violence and pessimism about Afghanistan's future in
some quarters, tens of thousands of men, women, and children who would not
have survived continued Taliban rule are alive today because of the partnership
between the Afghan people, health care providers and the international
community.
— Dr. Suraya Dalil, Afghan Minister of Public Health
On the Road to Recovery

Unlike Iraq, whose health system prior to decades of war beginning in the 1980s

was considered one of the finest in the Middle East, Afghanistan has never had a well-

functioning health system which effectively provided care to its citizens. With the

Communist takeover in 1978 and the decades of war that followed, the Afghan health

system steadily deteriorated so that by the time of the U.S. intervention in 2001, it was in

complete disarray. This chapter examines the reconstruction and development of the

Afghan health care system since the overthrow of the Taliban in 2001.

The Afghan Health Care System Prior to
the Fall of the Taliban

Since the communist seizure of power in 1978, Afghanistan has suffered through

decades of nearly continuous war which have devastated the country's infrastructure and

left over one million of its citizens dead.[1] By the time the Taliban was ousted from power

in late 2001, Afghanistan ranked "at or near the bottom of every socioeconomic indicator

used to measure human and economic progress."[2] During the 1980s and 1990s, the

majority of the health care provided to Afghans living in rural areas, where more than

80 percent of the population lived, was provided by NGOs.[3] Overall coverage was not

very good with only approximately one health care facility for every 50,000 people.[4] There was generally little coordination between NGOs and even less government oversight. As in Iraq, many of Afghanistan's health care professionals departed the country during these decades due to the poor security situation.

During the Taliban's rule, the country's health system deteriorated rapidly. Hospitals were frequently shut down, medical supplies were generally unavailable, and female physicians and nurses were forbidden to work.[5] The female population of the country therefore had little access to medical care since cultural norms generally prohibit male physicians from treating females. Average life expectancy in 2001 was 43 years, the lowest in the region. The provision of primary health care services throughout the country was exceedingly low, with only 6 percent of births involving skilled birth attendants, a prenatal care coverage rate of 4.6 percent, and a child immunization coverage rate of less than 20 percent in rural areas.[6] Overall, the country had only a handful of functioning hospitals with few trained physicians, and the modern medical facilities that did exist were reserved almost exclusively for the urban elites while the huge majority of the poor in rural areas did without. At that time, Afghanistan faced some of the worst health statistics ever recorded, including an infant mortality rate of 165 per 1000 live births and 1600 maternal deaths for every 100,000 live births.[7] Over 25 percent of children died before their fifth birthday and over 60 percent of the population did not have access to any form of health care.[8]

Several factors which contributed significantly to the deplorable state of Afghanistan's health system would complicate the reconstruction and development effort that began after the removal of the Taliban. First, Afghanistan's extreme poverty contributed to the poor nutrition of its children and the lack of infrastructure, including health infrastructure. Second, insecurity limited the ability of Afghanistan's few health care professionals to reach the population, particularly in rural areas. Third, geographic inaccessibility further isolated the rural population. Fourth, Afghan cultural traditions had powerful influences on the manner in which health care was delivered, and in many ways constrained the development of the Afghan health system. In particular, gender attitudes limited opportunities for female medical personnel and frequently contributed to poor health care for women. Beliefs about the proper role of women in society likely contributed to higher female mortality from disease, including tuberculosis, and to high rates of maternal, child, and infant mortality.[9] Finally, unlike Iraq, the central government of Afghanistan had no history of providing health care to the nation as a whole, particularly to the rural areas. As result, the Afghan health system lacked leadership and capacity.[10]

A Growing Insurgency (December 2001 to December 2007)

Following the overthrow of the Taliban regime in 2001, the U.S. worked together with the UN and other organizations to begin the reconstruction and development of the Afghan health system. The U.S. effort was initially led by USAID in conjunction with the DOS and the DOD.[11] As in Iraq, the initial priority was humanitarian relief in order to prevent famine and epidemics. These initial efforts were successful in that neither famine, nor epidemics of disease, nor large flows of refugees ensued.

Basic Package of Health Services

Unlike in Iraq, effective planning concerning the health system at the national level began shortly after the departure of the Taliban and the establishment of the Transitional Islamic State of Afghanistan. In March 2002, the Afghan Ministry of Public Health (MOPH), working together with various U.S. government agencies, the UN, International Governmental Organizations, and NGOs, began a process to determine the major priorities for rebuilding the Afghan national health system. In so doing, it sought to identify those health services which should be available to all Afghans, even those living in remote and poor areas.[12] The U.S. Army and other coalition militaries played a very peripheral role in this process. These essential services were termed the Basic Package of Health Services (BPHS). The goal in developing them was to provide a standardized group of basic services to form the core of health care delivery in all primary care facilities in Afghanistan.

In developing the BPHS, the Afghan MOPH and its partners sought to include those basic services which would have the greatest impact on major health problems. The new package was designed to be cost-effective, to extend coverage into remote and rural areas, and to provide a foundation for a new Afghan health system focused on public health and community-based primary care.[13] The initial version of the BPHS was adopted and published by the MOPH in March 2003. This package addressed seven important programs which form the foundation of good public health: maternal and newborn health, child health and immunization, public nutrition, communicable diseases, mental health, disability, and the supply of essential drugs.[14] The BPHS clearly delineated which services should be provided by each type of primary health care facility in the Afghan health system, and furthermore specified the staff, equipment, diagnostic services, and medications required to provide those services.

The initial BPHS was too ambitious and did not include benchmarks or cost budgeting. In response, over 100 international experts compiled a report published in 2005 which addressed many of these shortfalls.[15] It provided costs for all the goals listed in the plan, milestones for 2006 and 2015, and recommendations concerning the future transition to sustainability. The establishment of the BPHS was crucial in the reconstruction and development of the Afghan health system because it brought coherence and unified the priorities of the health system after decades of war. In addition, it provided a roadmap and sense of direction for all of the organizations working in the health sector. All NGOs and other organizations delivering health services in Afghanistan were required to work with the MOPH to ensure that their programs fulfilled the requirements of the BPHS. It also ensured that public health and primary health care would be the basis of the Afghan health system. In 2005, the Afghan MOPH developed the Essential Package of Health Services (EPHS), which was modeled upon the BPHS and focused on standardizing and improving the quality of hospital services provided to the population of Afghanistan.

Because of the complete lack of trained personnel, infrastructure, and resources in the years immediately after the overthrow of the Taliban, the Afghan MOPH, in consultation with its partners, made the decision to contract with NGOs to deliver primary care services to the vast majority of the Afghan population. The European Union, USAID, and the World Bank were the primary donors who funded these contracts. By 2008, 82 percent of the Afghan population lived in districts where primary care services were provided by NGOs under contract with the MOPH.[16] Each NGO was contracted to provide the BPHS as defined by the MOPH in a given area (usually a province). The approximate cost of delivering the BPHS was $4 per capita per year in 2008, a modest amount in comparison with the experience in other poor countries.[17]

The Afghan MOPH and its partners also made a significant commitment to independent monitoring and evaluation of health system performance via household surveys, health care facility assessments, and an improved health management information system. The initial results reported in 2007 were encouraging. The number of functioning primary health care facilities grew from 496 facilities in 2002 to 1169 facilities in 2007, with an increase in the proportion of those facilities with female medical personnel increasing from 24.8 percent to 83.0 percent.[18] In addition, there were increases in the number of outpatient visits, immunization rates for children, and prenatal care visits. The infant mortality rate decreased from 165 per 1000 live births in 2002 to 129 in 2006.[19] Despite these improvements, there were some critics of the Afghan MOPH's decision to engage in long-term contracting with NGOs. For instance, Doctors Without Borders, which withdrew from Afghanistan in July 2004 after several of its members were killed, asserted that this approach was not sustainable in the long-term and retarded the development of host nation personnel and facilities. The issue of sustainability is the fundamental one and only time will tell whether the Afghan people will be able to successfully take over once the NGOs depart. However, given the deplorable conditions faced by the Afghan MOPH in 2002, there was really no other choice which would have provided a realistic path towards successful reconstruction and development other than through contracting with NGOs.

Initial U.S. Army and Provincial
Reconstruction Team Efforts

In the immediate aftermath of the Taliban's overthrow, there were two camps within the U.S. government concerning the appropriate size and mission of U.S. forces in Afghanistan.[20] The side which included Secretary of Defense Donald Rumsfeld and U.S. Central Command Commander Tommy Franks favored a "light footprint" with a small force located only in Kabul. This side eventually won out over those who advocated a larger force spread throughout the country and involved in development projects. Ultimately, the U.S. deployed 8000 troops to Afghanistan in 2002 with a mission to hunt Taliban and Al Qaeda members, while the 4000 member international peacekeeping force in Kabul did not leave the city limits.[21] Over the next several years, as the war in Iraq grew in size, the focus of the U.S. military would shift to Iraq while the mission in Afghanistan would always come second. As the war in Afghanistan progressed, there were never enough troops or civilian experts in Afghanistan to accomplish the necessary tasks and as a result the insurgency grew progressively stronger. By 2008, there were just over 30,000 U.S. troops in Afghanistan while there were over 140,000 in Iraq. This light footprint "translated into one of the lowest levels of troops, police, and financial assistance in any stabilization operation since the end of World War II."[22]

As a result of the inadequate numbers of troops and civilian experts, the U.S. military and coalition forces were able to clear territories of insurgents temporarily but could not then hold them. There were also far too few troops available to provide assistance with development and the restoration of essential services, including health, throughout the wide expanses of rural Afghanistan. As a result, weak local, district, and provincial governments throughout Afghanistan were unable to provide essential services or security to local Afghans, especially in rural areas. This failure of governance in rural areas throughout Afghanistan, but particularly in southern and eastern Afghanistan, opened the door to the resurgence of the Taliban and other insurgent groups. Between 2002 and 2006, the number of insurgent initiated attacks increased 400 percent and by 2006, a full-fledged insurgency existed in Afghanistan.[23] Also in 2006, the North Atlantic Treaty Organization (NATO) assumed responsibility for security across the whole of Afghanistan by formally expanding its mission to the south. By 2007, international forces in Afghanistan were divided into five regional commands.

U.S. Army medical personnel at the tactical and operational levels generally had little or no guidance concerning the role they should play in the reconstruction and development of the Afghan health system during this period. There was no linkage in most cases with the Afghan MOPH and no military efforts to develop the BPHS in areas of rural Afghanistan where U.S. troops were based.[24] There was a complete impasse between strategic level planning in Kabul on the one hand, and Army medical personnel and tactical units on the ground on the other. As a result, for the first five years of U.S. involvement many units fell back on their old standby, the MEDCAP, and other forms of short-term, ad hoc direct patient care to Afghan villagers. During this period, Army medical personnel at the tactical level generally did not work together with Afghan MOPH officials to build medical capacity and improve governance at the local level, despite the overwhelming need. As in Iraq, too often CERP funds were used to build clinics and purchase expensive medical equipment which ended up going unused because prior consultation with host nation officials had not been done.

PRTs were first implemented in Afghanistan in 2002. By 2008, there were 12

PRTs under U.S. control and 15 PRTs controlled by other NATO countries throughout

Afghanistan.[25] American-led PRTs in Afghanistan differed from those in Iraq in that the

lead authority was a military officer and staffing was heavily weighted toward military

personnel, with only three to five civilians on a team of 50 to 100 individuals. PRTs in

Afghanistan normally co-located with combat units. The medical personnel on U.S.-led

PRTs normally included a physician assistant, one Non-Commissioned Officer, and two

medics, none of whom generally had any training or expertise in health system

reconstruction and development. During this time period, PRTs in Afghanistan were

subject to many of the same criticisms as those in Iraq, including that they were focused

exclusively on short-term projects, lacked strategic objectives, and had no metrics to

measure effectiveness.

However, the most important factor limiting the effectiveness of PRTs overseen

by both NATO and the U.S. is that five years after the overthrow of the Taliban, they had

very little operational reach into rural areas. PRTs operated in virtually all Afghan cities,

but their activities were largely restricted to urban areas due to security conditions.[26] This

inability of coalition military units and PRTs to operate effectively in rural areas

throughout Afghanistan in order to build effective governance, security, and

development, including health system reconstruction and development, was the key

factor in the growth of the insurgency throughout rural areas of Afghanistan. This was

particularly true of Afghanistan's southern and eastern regions.

During this period, the Defense Department also invested hundreds of millions of

dollars in order to develop a health system for the Afghan National Security Forces

(ANSF), including the Afghan National Army and Afghan National Police. Unfortunately, the lack of integration and coordination between civilian and military organizations, as well as between various branches of the Afghan and U.S. militaries, meant that much of this money was wasted in stovepiped projects with significant duplication of effort. In a review conducted in 2007, the DOD's Deputy Inspector General concluded that a sustainable ANSF health care system depended upon achieving an integrated Afghan civil–military–police health care system, with the ANSF supported by civilian clinical services, medical education, and medical logistics.[27] However, the Deputy Inspector General found that the lack of coordination and long-term planning by the U.S. Central Command, ISAF, Combined Security Transition Command-Afghanistan, and the U.S. Mission–Afghanistan, significantly hindered progress in this area. He also found that the majority of U.S. and NATO-ISAF medical mentoring teams were not fully manned or adequately trained. Furthermore, restrictive personnel practices for the U.S. Navy and U.S. Air Force medical personnel assigned to Combined Security Transition Command-Afghanistan seriously hindered its ability to relocate them to meet requirements throughout Afghanistan. The Deputy Inspector General concluded that U.S. Central Command, in coordination with the U.S. Mission–Afghanistan, Afghan medical leadership, NATO–ISAF, and multiple interagency and international partners, "needs to develop a comprehensive, integrated, multi-year plan to build a sustainable ANSF health care system."[28]

Unity of Command and Unity of Effort

Challenges with attaining unity of command and unity of effort pervaded U.S. involvement with reconstruction and development of the Afghan health system. The presence of multiple military headquarters and the division of U.S. forces between Operation Enduring Freedom and NATO-ISAF complicated efforts to integrate and synchronize the efforts of military medical personnel from different countries. The same institutional arrangements which complicated interagency coordination in Iraq affected relationships between military units and civilian organizations in Afghanistan as well. There was no effective mechanism for coordination and integration of the various organizations working on health system reconstruction and development. In addition, the lack of a lead actor during various phases of the war significantly hindered the development of effective unity of effort.

The Adoption of Counterinsurgency Tactics
(January 2008 to December 2011)

The growing strength of the insurgency in Afghanistan, the realization that the strategies and tactics employed over the previous six years had been largely unsuccessful, and the success of counterinsurgency tactics in Iraq all contributed to the adjustments in strategy which began in 2007 to 2008. The drawdown in Iraq eventually freed up significant numbers of U.S. troops for deployment to Afghanistan beginning in 2009. These additional forces finally began to provide the minimal numbers of troops necessary to wage a counterinsurgency campaign. Preliminary data was beginning to show an overall improvement in Afghanistan's health system but many rural areas, particularly in less secure southern and eastern parts of the country, had failed to see much progress. This lack of progress in remote and insecure areas likely reflected the absence of development assistance from coalition military forces, PRTs, and local Afghan governments in these regions.

U.S. Military Efforts

The 82nd Airborne Division, organized as Coalition Joint Task Force-82 (CJTF-82), was one of the first units in Afghanistan, and certainly the first conventional unit, to wage a comprehensive and successful counterinsurgency campaign within its area of operations. During previous tours in 2002 and 2004, they had earned a reputation as "door kickers," focused on killing bad guys. But over the course of a 15 month tour beginning in January 2007, Major General David Rodriguez' Task Force focused on reconstruction and development projects throughout Regional Command-East.[29] One of their key lessons learned was that security improvements occur when the population sees growth in governmental capacity and tangible development efforts. In other words, "good governance leads to good security."[30]

The CJTF-82 surgeon's section developed a health sector strategy which was in complete alignment with the Afghan MOPH's own strategy involving the implementation of the BPHS. The overall goal of the CJTF-82 strategy was to develop confidence and support for the government of Afghanistan within the Afghan population through improved health care. They also sought to connect the districts and provinces to the national level of government.[31] The CJTF-82 surgeon's section began with an analysis of actions taken in the health sector over the previous five years in order to identify what had worked and what had not. They identified three areas which required transformation. First, a change from short-term projects to long-term programs which were sustainable was required to develop capacity and self-reliance. Second, the provision of direct patient care to Afghan citizens by U.S. and other coalition health care providers via MEDCAPs needed to be stopped. It was doing nothing to develop capacity or promote confidence on the part of the Afghan people in the local government and MOPH. Third, a focused change from building large-scale infrastructure to increasing intellectual capacity was necessary. The overarching objective of CJTF-82 was described as emphasizing "Facilitate and Empower" rather than "Perform and Do."[32]

The CJTF-82 plan called for subordinate units to conduct medical engagements, training events, and team leader meetings at all government levels from the village to the province in support of the MOPH's strategy to implement the BPHS. Military providers in maneuver units and PRTs were specifically tasked to partner with the communities in their battle spaces to improve the Afghan health system and infrastructure. CJTF-82 units were involved in training programs for midwives and other capacity- building workshops. They were also extensively involved with teaching medical skills to the ANSF and sought to leverage U.S. military international partners (Jordanians, Koreans, and Egyptians) to change past humanitarian practices to reflect the new practice of mentoring Afghans, and to conduct side by side training to further build capability and capacity. CJTF-82 units worked closely with Afghan MOPH officials to develop a responsive medical logistics system along with disease surveillance and outbreak response systems. Finally, subordinate units were tasked to perform ongoing village medical assessments involving the availability of clean drinking water, facility evaluations, and preventive medicine programs in order to capture community health needs.[33]

Because there were no USAID or Department of Health and Human Services civilian representatives at the local, district, or provincial level to mentor Afghan health leaders, CJTF-82 medical personnel performed this job in their place. The CJTF-82 strategy recommended placement of USAID and Department of Health and Human

Services representatives at lower levels of government in mentorship roles, and also recommended an expansion of the medical section of the PRT to include a senior medical provider and a medical service operations officer to coordinate projects. Throughout all of CJTF-82's written documents and actions, the Afghan MOPH was recognized as the lead agency in directing health care efforts in Afghanistan.[34]

Under the leadership of CJTF-82, eastern Afghanistan appeared to rebound in 2008. Whereas only approximately 10 percent of Afghans in the east had access to basic health care in 2004, by 2008 more than 75 percent did.[35] However, it is important to note that eastern Afghanistan represented only one of five regional commands in Afghanistan, and none of the other regional commands were at that time implementing widespread counterinsurgency strategies or having that kind of success. In fact, the British government, which controlled Regional Command-South, went out of its way to assert that eastern Afghanistan was easier terrain for counterinsurgency and that successful approaches there were not transferable to the south. It was another example of the lack of unity of effort that was all too common throughout the war.

While the 82nd Airborne Division is a prime example of a conventional unit which had success in Afghanistan employing the unconventional tactics of counterinsurgency, the small teams which make up the unconventional Army Special Forces have a long history of successful counterinsurgency operations. No other unit spent as much time day-to-day, on the ground, working shoulder to shoulder with the population as the 12-man Special Forces Operational Detachment Alpha. The prolonged intimacy that Special Forces teams develop with local villagers serves as the foundation for their success in the fundamentals of counterinsurgency, including building security, governance, and development. For Special Forces units in Afghanistan, the best solutions were local ones, developed by the Afghans themselves, and the only effective way to build the Afghan government was from the bottom-up in the villages. Village Stability Operations were one method employed by Special Forces units throughout Afghanistan. According to one Operational Detachment Alpha Commander, "The Village Stability Operations methodology is a bottom-up approach that employs U.S. Special Operations Forces teams and partnered units embedded with villagers in order to establish security and to support and promote socio-economic development and good governance."[36]

Medical personnel assigned to Special Forces units in Afghanistan also developed innovative ways of engaging the population at the grassroots level as a means of improving public health and health care delivery in remote and insecure areas, where the insurgency was most powerful. For example, Major Shawn Alderman, the battalion surgeon for 2nd Battalion, 1st Special Forces Group (Airborne), along with the battalion's other medical personnel, developed the concept of Medical Seminars (MEDSEMs) during their service in the Philippines. They then transported the concept to Afghanistan in 2010, while serving in some of the most conflicted parts of Regional Command-South.[37] MEDSEMs are medical operations designed to connect isolated populations to their government while providing sustainable, medically sound interventions which improve public health.

Whereas MEDCAPs involve the provision of direct patient care by U.S. doctors to local villagers and may undermine counterinsurgency objectives by reducing the confidence the population has in their own local government's ability to meet their health care needs, MEDSEMs turn the MEDCAP concept on its head in support of counterinsurgency principles. MEDSEMs are completely led by local national officials and are facilitated by coalition forces. They are designed to promote interoperability between local Afghan leaders, Afghan medical officials, and Afghan security forces. The key to their success is a prolonged period of area preparation and relationship building which occurs over 30 to 60 days. During this period there are multiple planning meetings which foster relationship building and information sharing between participants. This first phase is followed by phase two, the actual execution of the medical seminar over three to four days. The seminar features classroom instruction by local Afghan medical officials on public health topics focused on basic women's and children's health to Afghan villagers. The event is hosted by local government officials and security is provided by ANSF. The event concludes with student-led medical engagements in which students assist local medical officials in surrounding villages. Phase three, the final phase, involves follow-up and relationship maintenance indefinitely into the future. During this phase the MEDSEM graduates serve as volunteer assistants in local clinics and facilitate future medical interventions and engagements under the mentorship of local medical providers.[38]

According to Alderman, medical programs in counterinsurgencies can be valuable tools when they properly align with operational objectives. MEDSEMs are a way for commanders to influence operationally important geographical areas or populations in order to meet the desired end state. By fully integrating host nation assets, ensuring that host nation officials are at the forefront at all times, promoting the capacity of the host nation government, and enabling self-sufficiency, MEDSEMs improve governance and the confidence of the people in their own government. MEDSEMs connect local doctors, nurses, midwives, and recently trained villagers to their local population with the intent of increasing the perception by villagers that local MOPH officials and medical personnel are responsible for their health and have their best interests in mind.[39]

The 2nd Battalion, 1st Special Forces Group (Airborne) had significant success in implementing the MEDSEM concept throughout southern Afghanistan in 2010. They obtained support for the concept from a wide cross-section of organizations throughout Afghanistan including ISAF, the Afghan MOPH, Regional Command-South, USAID, the Kandahar and Zabul PRTs, and numerous NGOs. They also worked closely with Afghan MOPH officials to ensure that all of their efforts were completely aligned with MOPH strategic plans. Many of the events featured an opening ceremony with an introductory address by the provincial Director of Public Health in the area. Over time, as a result of regular meetings between the unit's medical personnel and local MOPH officials, MEDSEMs became more closely aligned with the MOPH policy to place Community Health Workers in isolated villages and featured instruction based on the official Afghan Community Health Worker program.[40]

MEDEMs were particularly successful in activating and empowering the MOPH in rural villages of southern Afghanistan where they had not been previously active due to the security situation and the influence of the insurgency. Special Forces medical personnel also worked closely with USAID during these MEDSEMs and they thus served as a mechanism for USAID to become involved in areas where they had previously been unable to work due to poor security.[41]

Finally, Alderman and his team were able to do something that very few medical personnel involved in medical operations in either Iraq or Afghanistan were able to do:

they developed relevant measures of performance and more importantly measures of effectiveness aligned with their objectives and then tracked the effects on the population that their MEDSEMs were having over time. Measures of effectiveness were tracked across seven different lines of operation: capacity to govern, security, access, interoperability, focused engagement, medical, and information operations. Preliminary reports of measures in multiple categories taken 45 days after the first event in one district supported the idea that MEDSEMs were making a difference. There was improved attendance at district shuras, increased Improvised Explosive Device reporting by local nationals, increased white space around the district, and multiple requests by tribal leaders for additional medical engagements.[42]

This use of measures of effectiveness by 2nd Battalion, 1st Special Forces Group (Airborne) in an effort to establish metrics for identifying just which medical operations were successful and should be expanded versus which should be discontinued, was unfortunately far too rare. The ongoing failure of military medical personnel and PRTs to develop effective metrics for determining which types of medical operations had the desired effects, and then to track those metrics closely over time, was a huge factor in the inability of U.S. medical counterinsurgents to learn as the war progressed.

Although Alderman's Special Forces Battalion did great work in some of the most insecure districts of southern Afghanistan, there were far more villages and districts which were not engaged by the Afghan MOPH, coalition military units, or PRTs. An examination of after action reviews from many units throughout Afghanistan active at this time provides only sporadic evidence that their medical personnel were effectively engaged in medical civil-military relations or health system reconstruction and development. Furthermore, given the economy of force, ISAF and the U.S. military had to make difficult decisions about priorities of effort. One area in the health sector which continued to receive a large percentage of U.S. dollars and manpower was the development of the ANSF health system. By 2010, the U.S. Medical Training Advisory Group included 155 U.S. military medical mentors throughout Afghanistan who worked in the offices of the Surgeons General for both the Afghan National Police and the Afghan National Army. They also worked in the National Military Hospital in Kabul and in regional military hospitals in other cities.[43] The U.S. Medical Training Advisory Group oversaw the construction of five 50-bed hospitals exclusively for the use of ANSF and had a budget of approximately $130 or $140 million per year, not including infrastructure costs, solely for equipment, pharmaceuticals, and other necessities to support development of the ANSF health system.[44]

The issue with the U.S. decision to prioritize money and support for the Afghan military health system is that it did so at the expense of the Afghan civilian health system at a time when large areas of rural Afghanistan, particularly in the southern and eastern regions of the country where the insurgency was strongest, rarely if ever had contact with the Afghan MOPH, U.S. forces, or PRTs. This failure to attack the insurgent's center of gravity via support and development of the population in rural areas of the country that served as the insurgents' base remained a crucial driver of further insurgency. In addition, the continued lack of coordination and integration among the Afghan civilian health system, the Afghan National Army health system, and the Afghan National Police health system defied logic and is not sustainable once the U.S. and NATO depart. Events like the construction and reopening in 2009 of the Afghan Military Medical School, dedicated solely to the training of physicians for the Afghan military, are evidence of a failure of integration. Once again, the fact that there was no mechanism or body for coordination between civilian and military organizations working in the respective health systems led to duplication of effort and wasted money. The prioritization of resources for military health systems tends to create the multitiered health systems not uncommon in poor countries in which the military health system far outclasses the underfunded and second-class civilian health system.[45]

The year 2009 represented a pivotal year for U.S. and coalition forces in Afghanistan with the appointment of General Stanley McChrystal as ISAF Commander, the codification of the change in strategy represented by McChrystal's ISAF Commander's Counterinsurgency Guidance, and a decision by President Obama to surge 30,000 additional troops. All of these events represented a recognition of the fact that the ISAF strategy was not working and that the insurgency was growing in strength. In his guidance, McChrystal directed ISAF forces away from conventional tactics and towards an embrace of the Afghan people, with a focus on building governance capacity and accountability at all levels down to local communities.[46] General Petraeus went one step farther the next year in his guidance, recommending that ISAF forces "live with the people."[47] The subsequent actions and directives of both the PRTs and ISAF medical officials reflect this change in direction.

The Evolution of Provincial Reconstruction Teams in Afghanistan

By 2010, there were 27 ISAF PRTs in Afghanistan, including 12 belonging to the U.S. Though PRTs in Afghanistan initially faced criticism for their focus on short-term,

100

unsustainable construction projects, over time most critics acknowledged that PRTs moved towards support for more long-term, capacity-building efforts. The 2009 ISAF PRT handbook reflects this with its focus on the four enduring principles which underpinned all of its operations in reconstruction and development: Afghan-owned, ISAF-enabled, wholly collaborative and sustainable.[48] It focused on operationalizing these principles in the health sector via engagement with the Afghan MOPH at the national level and the application of military medical resources at the local level. However, the dearth of medical personnel assigned to PRTs severely limited their ability to make meaningful contributions to health system reconstruction and development. In addition, their ability to work in the insecure areas of southern and eastern Afghanistan, where the insurgency was most powerful, remained severely constrained.

International Security Assistance Force Position
on Military Medical Engagements

In July 2010, ISAF released its *Guidance on Military Medical Engagement in Health Sector Reconstruction and Development*. The document reflected a decade's worth of experiences on the part of ISAF nations in the reconstruction and development of the Afghan health system, including the initial failures with direct patient care by ISAF medical personnel and subsequent success with strategies based upon counterinsurgency principles. The document begins by asserting that the primary responsibility for health sector reconstruction and development rests with Afghan government, particularly the MOPH, and that ISAF military units and PRTs play a supporting role only. It goes on to discuss the reciprocal relationship between security and improved health care. Improving health care depends on the existence of secure conditions under which health care

101

providers can act. At the same time, improved health care capability reinforces security conditions by enhancing community support for the legitimacy of the government and reducing support for insurgents.[49] The document also states that the direct provision of health care by military personnel to Afghan citizens is generally detrimental to the long-term development of the Afghan health system and it therefore asserts that MEDCAPs do more harm than good.

The guidance goes on to say that military involvement in health sector reconstruction and development should always be based upon a direct request from the Afghan MOPH and that civilians should have primacy over health sector reconstruction and development. All medical engagements in which military units participate should have Afghan health care professionals at the forefront and should be Afghan-owned, delivered to Afghan standards, and sustainable.[50] Finally, the document acknowledges the need for the development of improved measures of performance and measures of effectiveness during the planning for any medical engagement. This guidance reflects how many important lessons were learned over the first decade of ISAF involvement in Afghanistan and establishes a firm groundwork for future military medical engagements by ISAF countries.[51]

In 2011, the ISAF medical section began to focus on transitioning towards its desired end-state: an Afghan government capable of assuming and sustaining execution of medical operations.[52] ISAF's engagement strategy reflected the important lessons learned over the previous decade about the right way to do health system reconstruction and development during counterinsurgency. ISAF's initiatives (plans, programs, and operations), capabilities (knowledge and training), and resources (materials, facilities, and services) were all focused on support for the Afghan MOPH's development efforts. All ISAF medical operations now had to pass a six question test:

1. Is it necessary to establish an essential system or service?

2. Is it culturally appropriate?

3. Is it supported by the Afghan government?

4. Is it executable?

5. Is it affordable (in the long-term)?

6. Is it sustainable?[53]

ISAF's support was focused increasingly on public health programs such as the Community Led Total Sanitation Program used in Village Stability Operations and community development councils, a Polio Eradication Campaign, and a National Burn Campaign focused on the prevention of burns to children.[54] It also focused on human capacity building via mentoring and training of the ANSF with the goal of a competent and self-sustained ANSF medical service, capable of independent support of ANSF operations. On the civilian side, ISAF training programs used only MOPH-approved standards and curricula and focused on training the Afghan trainer. Its civilian physician assistant and nurse training programs were geared toward increasing the rural postings of these medical professionals.[55] All of these initiatives were evidence of the significant progress ISAF and the U.S. military had made in developing programs which were medically sound, host nation-led, capacity-building, sustainable, and aligned with counterinsurgency principles.

Experiences with Implementing Counterinsurgency Tactics
in Afghanistan

Several important lessons learned have grown out of recent experiences with implementing counterinsurgency tactics throughout Afghanistan, in the health sector as well as in other lines of operation. First, the efforts in Afghanistan of the U.S. Government as a whole, including both civilian and military organizations, have been delivered in too much of a top-down fashion rather than from a bottom-up approach. The vast majority of money, personnel, emphasis, and projects have all gone to and through Kabul where they have been subject to all kinds of misdirection and corruption, rather than directly to local communities in rural areas of Afghanistan. Two-thirds of U.S. government civilians in Afghanistan work in Kabul. The failure of the U.S. to prioritize improved governance and development in rural areas of Afghanistan, particularly in regions of southern and eastern Afghanistan which serve as the base for the insurgency, has allowed the insurgency to continue to grow despite increased numbers of troops and billions of dollars spent.[56]

Afghanistan is a rurally based society and its insurgency is "rooted in the political, economic, and social dynamics of rural areas."[57] Many of the rural areas of southern and eastern Afghanistan have been wracked by violence and insecurity and, as a result, have remained mainly off-limits to NGOs and other civilian organizations. Unfortunately, for too long ISAF and the U.S. military did not prioritize the placement of troops, the development of good governance, and the delivery of essential services in these areas. On those occasions when U.S. Army medical personnel have engaged local populations in these areas via innovative medical operations based on counterinsurgency principles, they have been quite successful. Overall though, despite GEN Petraeus' injunction to "live among the people," the majority of U.S. Army and ISAF troops for many years remained largely isolated on well-fortified Forward Operating Bases while most U.S. Government civilians remained in Kabul. Meanwhile, the insurgency continued to thrive in villages that were mainly out of the reach of the Afghan Government and coalition military forces.

U.S. Army medical personnel had the most success when they worked side-by-side in local communities with the population and with Afghan MOPH officials, developing relationships while building capacity, improving governance, and tying the population to their government. Medical personnel from the 82nd Airborne Division and the 2nd Battalion, 1st Special Forces Group (Airborne) validated this concept in their operations. In counterinsurgency generally, and in health system reconstruction and development during counterinsurgency in particular, how people are engaged may be more important than what is produced.[58] Engaging in health system reconstruction and development during counterinsurgency, like all counterinsurgency work, is incredibly difficult and too often units and commanders fall back on conventional methods and force protection. In order to be successful, units need to engage the population, live among the people, develop innovative programs, and build capacity in the areas where the insurgency is strongest.

One other important lesson learned is that too much aid can in many ways be destabilizing.[59] The billions of dollars poured into Afghanistan by the U.S. and other countries have destabilized Afghanistan's fragile economy and political system by "fueling corruption, supporting a lucrative economy that benefits insurgents, and creating perverse incentives among key actors to maintain the status quo of insecurity and bad governance."[60] In the health sector, those programs that have been most successful have been focused on capacity building and tailored to the public health and primary care focus of Afghanistan's BPHS. Meanwhile, the hundreds of millions of dollars spent on advanced medical equipment and unwanted medical facilities have largely been wasted.

<u>Overview of Afghan Health System</u>
<u>Reconstruction and Development</u>

At the time of the overthrow of the Taliban in 2001, Afghanistan was one of the poorest countries in the world with a completely dysfunctional health system, one in far poorer condition than the Iraqi health system at a similar juncture. Despite this, the Afghan MOPH in conjunction with numerous international health organizations quickly developed an effective national strategic plan built around the BPHS that was public health and primary care-oriented. It was also designed to reach underserved rural populations. The most recent survey data shows that in many ways health system reconstruction and development over the previous decade has been quite successful.

The Afghanistan Mortality Survey, conducted in 2010, found that most Afghans are living longer, fewer newborns are dying, and far more women are surviving childbirth as a result of the dramatic improvements in Afghanistan's health system over the past decade.[61] Life expectancy has improved from 43 years in 2000 to between 62 and 64 years for both men and women.[62] Infant mortality has declined from 165 deaths per 1000 live births in 2000 to 97.[63] In addition, the number of health care facilities in Afghanistan improved from 450 in 2003 to more than 1800, while the number of trained midwives grew from 400 to 2000.[64] There are also now more than 20,000 trained Community Health Workers.[65] However, one very important caveat must be noted in regards to the survey data. While the survey covered 87 percent of Afghanistan, this included 98

percent of the urban population but only 84 percent of the rural population.[66] Most

importantly, for security reasons it did not include rural areas of the three major southern

provinces (Kandahar, Helmand, and Zabul) which are the base of the insurgency.

This failure to include data from the provinces in southern Afghanistan where the

insurgency is strongest is a reflection of the failure, until recently, of the Afghan

government and its many partners, including the U.S. and ISAF, to effectively engage the

population in these areas in an effort to improve security, governance, and development.

The inability of the U.S. Army and other organizations to do effective health system

reconstruction and development (and other forms of development) for too many years in

the areas where the Taliban was strongest was largely the result of too few troops and at

times misplaced priorities. Developing an effective national strategy, as occurred with the

creation of the BPHS, is an essential and necessary first step for effective health system

reconstruction and development but it is not sufficient. The inability to fully implement

the BPHS in the areas where it was most needed for success in counterinsurgency

illustrates the essential role that the lack of security played in preventing local

government officials and civilian organizations from operating in crucial areas of the

country. In these areas it was primarily left to military organizations to step in, and in the

vast majority of cases they did not for the first six or seven years of conflict. By the time

they began to engage the population in these conflicted areas of particularly southern

Afghanistan, they were forced to try to come from far behind in battling a well-

established insurgency. However, over the last several years, some impressive strides

have been made with the adoption of strategies based on counterinsurgency principles.

There have been several examples of effective medical operations by units in Afghanistan, including the 82nd Airborne Division and the 2nd Battalion, 1st Special Forces Group (Airborne). Unfortunately, though, there are not enough other examples from throughout the country. These units established an effective model of medical operations performed in alignment with counterinsurgency operational objectives. The success of these operations, like the Village Stability Operations implemented by Special Forces units and others, demonstrates the importance of engaging the population via bottom-up strategies focused at the local and district level in a rurally-based society like Afghanistan. In addition, it is essential that these local and tactical operations are nested with and tied to operational and strategic planning at higher levels.[67]

A retrospective analysis of the entire course of Afghan health system reconstruction and development in light of the six principles discussed in chapter 3 which should serve to guide the process shows a significant degree of conformity with the principles. There was an effective transition from emergency relief to health system reconstruction and development. In addition, a comprehensive systems-based approach guided the process and there was a consistent focus on public health and primary care. Health system development largely remained centered in the community and the development of capacity was generally a priority.

Table 2 demonstrates the progress over time within the three health system building blocks which are the focus of this thesis: health service delivery, the health workforce, and leadership and governance of the health system. There was consistent progress within all three building blocks and particularly within the health service delivery block.

[2]Jones et al., *Securing Health: Lessons from Nation-Building Missions,* 189.

[3]Loevinsohn and Sayed, "Lessons from the Health Sector in Afghanistan: How Progress Can Be Made in Challenging Circumstances," 725.

[4]Ibid., 724.

[5]Jones et al., *Securing Health: Lessons from Nation-Building Missions,* 190.

[6]UNICEF and Central Statistics Office, Afghanistan Transitional Authority, "Multiple indicator cluster survey 2003 report for Afghanistan," http://www.childinfo.org/mics2_afghanistan.html (accessed 2 May 2012).

[7]Islamic Republic of Afghanistan Ministry of Public Health, "A Basic Package of Health Services for Afghanistan, 2005/1384," http://www.msh.org/afghanistan/pdf/Afghanistan_BPHS_2005_1384.pdf (accessed 2 May 2012), 1.

[8]Ibid.

[9]Jones et al., *Securing Health: Lessons from Nation-Building Missions,* 194.

[10]Ibid., 195.

[11]Ibid., 197.

[12]Islamic Republic of Afghanistan Ministry of Public Health, "A Basic Package of Health Services for Afghanistan, 2005/1384," 1.

[13]Ibid.

[14]Ibid., 14.

[15]Jones et al., *Securing Health: Lessons from Nation-Building Missions,* 201.

[16]Ibid., 199.

[17]Loevinsohn and Sayed, "Lessons from the Health Sector in Afghanistan: How Progress Can Be Made in Challenging Circumstances," 725.

[18]Ibid.

[19]Ibid.

[20]Seth G. Jones, *In the Graveyard of Empires: America's War in Afghanistan* (New York: W.W. Norton and Company 2009), 112.

[21]Ibid., 115.

[22]Ibid., 118.

[23]Ibid., xxiii.

[24]MCM Bricknell, "Reflections on medical aspects of ISAF IX in Afghanistan," *JR Army Med Corps* 153, no. 1 (March 2007): 49-50.

[25]Robert J. Bebber, "The Role of Provincial Reconstruction Teams in Counterinsurgency Operations: Khost Province, Afghanistan," *Small Wars Journal* (10 November 2008), http://smallwarsjournal.com/blog/journal/docs-temp/131-bebber.pdf?q=mag/docs-temp/131-bebber.pdf (accessed 2 May 2012).

[26]Seth G. Jones, *In the Graveyard of Empires: America's War in Afghanistan* (New York: W.W. Norton and Company 2009), 302.

[27]Thomas F. Gimble, "Principal Deputy Inspector General Department of Defense before the House Oversight and Government Reform Committee Subcommittee on National Security and Foreign Affairs: DoD IG Assessment of Arms, Ammunition, and Explosives Control and Accountability; Security Assistance; and Sustainment for the Afghan National Security Forces," 12 February 2009, http://www.dodig.mil/ IGInformation/ Speeches/HOGR%202-12-09.pdf (accessed 2 May 2012), 7.

[28]Ibid., 8.

[29]Jones, *In the Graveyard of Empires: America's War in Afghanistan*, 297.

[30]CJTF-82, "Key Lessons Learned," (2008), http://lessonslearned.amedd. army.mil/ (accessed 11 February 2012).

[31]CJTF-82, "Surgeon AAR," (2008), http://lessonslearned.amedd.army.mil/ (accessed 11 February 2012).

[32]CJTF-82 Surgeon's Section, "Information Paper: CJTF-82 Health Sector Development in Afghanistan," (3 March 2008), http://lessonslearned.amedd.army.mil/ (accessed 11 February 2012), 3.

[33]Ibid., 1-11.

[34]Ibid.

[35]Jones, *In the Graveyard of Empires: America's War in Afghanistan*, 300.

[36]Rory Hanlin, "One Team's Approach to Village Stability Operations," *Small Wars Journal* (4 September 2011), http://smallwarsjournal.com/node/11412 (accessed 2 May 2012).

[37]Shawn Alderman, Jon Christensen, and Ingrham Crawford, "Medical Seminars: A New Paradigm for SOF Counterinsurgency Medical Programs," *Journal of Special Operations Medicine* 10, no. 1 (Winter 2010): 16-22.

[38]Ibid.

[39]Ibid.

[40]Authors' personal observations and conclusions.

[41]Authors' personal observations and conclusions.

[42]Authors' personal observations and conclusions.

[43]Federal News Service, "Department of Defense Bloggers Roundtable with COL Schuyler K. Geller, Command Surgeon and Commander, Medical Training Advisory Group, Camp Eggers, NATO Training Mission-Afghanistan/Combined Security Transition Command-Afghanistan," (23 June 2010), http://www.defense.gov/ Blog_files/Blog_assets/20100623_schuyler2_transcript.pdf (accessed 2 May 2012).

[44]Ibid.

[45]Donald F. Thompson, "The Role of Medical Diplomacy in Stabilizing Afghanistan," *Defense Horizons,* no. 63 (May 2008): 8.

[46]Small Wars Journal Editors, "ISAF Counterinsurgency Guidance Released," *Small Wars Journal,* 25 August 2009, http://smallwarsjournal.com/blog/isaf-counterinsurgency-guidance-released (accessed 2 May 2012).

[47]David Petraeus, "Multinational Force–Iraq Commander's Counterinsurgency Guidance," 2.

[48]International Security Assistance Force, *ISAF PRT Handbook*, 4th ed. (2009), https://www.cimicweb.org/Lists/PRT%20Handbook/AllItems.aspx (accessed 2 May 2012).

[49]Headquarters, International Security Assistance Force, "ISAF Guidance on Military Medical Engagement in Health Sector Reconstruction and Development," (28 July 2010).

[50]Ibid., 3.

[51]Ibid., 10-22.

[52]David J. Smith, "Health Sector Reconstruction and Development in ISAF," ISAF HQ, Kabul, Afghanistan (4 October 2011), http://95.110.200.129/act/images/ stories/events/2011/medconf/d1_smith.pdf (accessed 2 May 2012).

[53]Ibid.

[54]Ibid.

[55]Ibid.

[56]Ibid.

[57]Wilton Park Conference, "Winning Hearts and Minds in Afghanistan: Assessing the Effectiveness of Development and COIN Operations" (11-14 March 2010), http://www.eisf.eu/resources/library/1004WPCReport.pdf (accessed 2 May 2012).

[58]Ibid., 12.

[59]Ibid., 2.

[60]Ibid.

[61]Some sources have questioned the validity of the 2010 Afghanistan Mortality Survey data, given the large improvements over previous surveys. See Quil Lawrence, "Gains in Afghan Health: Too Good to be True?" *National Public Radio* (17 January 2012), http://www.npr.org/2012/01/17/145338803/gains-in-afghan-health-too-good-to-be-true (accessed 2 May 2012).

[62]Afghan Public Health Institute Ministry of Public Health, "Afghanistan Mortality Survey 2010," (November 2011), http://measuredhs.com/pubs/ pdf/FR248/FR248.pdf (accessed 2 May 2012), 124.

[63]Ibid., 91.

[64]Associated Press, "Afghanistan life expectancy rising as healthcare improves, survey shows," (30 November 2011), http://www.guardian.co.uk/world/2011/nov/30/ afghanistan-life-expectancy-rising-survey (accessed 2 May 2012).

[65]Ibid.

[66]Ibid.

[67]Simon Hamid, "Guidelines for Implementing Medical Operations in the Counterinsurgency (COIN) Fight: A Framework for Engagement," *Journal of Special Operations Medicine* 11, no. 2: 7-11.

CHAPTER 6

CONCLUSION AND RECOMMENDATIONS

If you want to go fast, you go alone. If you want to go far, you go with others.
— Dr. Suraya Dalil, Afghan Minister of Public Health
Health Sector Reconstruction and Development in ISAF

Conclusion

At the conclusion of major combat operations in both Iraq and Afghanistan, U.S. Army medical personnel confronted host nation health systems which were virtually collapsed. Together with host nation officials, other U.S. Government Agencies, NGOs, and international organizations, they took up the task of health system reconstruction and development. Army medical personnel assumed this effort in addition to what is always the primary and essential duty of all Army medical personnel in any combat environment: the treatment and evacuation of wounded American troops. The problem was that while American medical personnel were well-trained and well-resourced to care for American troops, they had absolutely no training, expertise, resources, or doctrine to guide them in health system reconstruction and development during what quickly turned into counterinsurgency in both countries. This occurred despite the fact that the last prolonged conflict in which the U.S. Army had been engaged was the nearly decade long Vietnam counterinsurgency and that since then the Army had provided support on a much smaller scale to counterinsurgency efforts in Central America and elsewhere. However, lessons learned concerning the medical aspects of counterinsurgency had not been institutionalized in doctrine or training after the Vietnam War or subsequently and instead were mainly lost to history.

114

Health system reconstruction and development in developing countries is difficult under the best of circumstances, even when done by humanitarian workers who are experts in the subject. It is significantly more complex in the aftermath of major combat operations and with a budding insurgency. Initial experiences in both Iraq and Afghanistan reflect these difficulties with frequent missteps as Army medical personnel and the other organizations involved in health system reconstruction and development tried to make the best of difficult situations. In Iraq, the lack of coordination and integration between the military and U.S. government agencies prior to the conflict and in the initial stages of post-conflict operations complicated the situation considerably. So too did the rapidly progressive deterioration in security which made it nearly impossible for civilian organizations to work in most areas of the country. As a result of the security situation, military units were frequently the only organizations capable of working at the local level for several years throughout the majority of the country.

In Afghanistan, effective planning at the national level did occur expeditiously after the end of major combat operations with the creation of the BPHS, a well-designed effort to bring preventive medicine and primary health care services to all of Afghanistan, including underserved rural areas. However, due to the very low number of troops for the first seven to eight years of the war and decisions concerning their prioritization, the population was generally not engaged for many years in large expanses of rural Afghanistan. Particularly in rural parts of the southern and eastern regions of the country where the insurgency was based, there was little reconstruction and development of the health system because coalition military forces and the Afghan MOPH were not active in those areas.

In both countries, initial efforts by military units and PRTs working on health system reconstruction and development were criticized on multiple accounts, including for their focus on short-term and expensive projects. Often, these costly projects included the purchase of large-scale infrastructure or medical equipment not appropriate for developing countries. In addition, there was little focus initially on capacity building or sustainability. Many expensive projects went unused because host nation medical officials were not consulted prior to initiation, and then not interested once they were complete. Finally, many medical personnel from Army units in the initial years after the end of major combat operations provided direct patient care to local villagers during MEDCAPs and similar operations, directly undermining the confidence of the population in the ability of their own government's medical officials and providers to care for them. In both Iraq and Afghanistan during the first five years after the end of major combat operations, the insurgency grew progressively stronger and though there were some minor improvements in each country's health system, overall health system reconstruction and development was not nearly as effective as it could have been.

However, in both countries things improved somewhat with the introduction of counterinsurgency doctrine and tactics, significant increases in the number of troops, and as Army medical personnel, PRTs, and other organizations learned about what worked and what did not when it came to health system reconstruction and development. According to the FM 3-24, the *Counterinsurgency* manual, the side that learns faster and adapts more rapidly, in other words the better learning organization, is the side that normally wins in a counterinsurgency campaign.[1] In both Iraq and Afghanistan, it took too long for the U.S. military to begin to adopt the appropriate counterinsurgency tactics and during this period the insurgency grew strong and developed significant influence over the population.

Success in counterinsurgency depends on the ability to build and maintain the legitimacy of the host nation government in the eyes of the people. In both Iraq and Afghanistan, Army medical personnel in some units were successful in implementing medical operations which were aligned with the principal counterinsurgency objectives. For example, as discussed in chapter 5, from 2005 to 2006 the 3rd ACR in Al Anbar Province Iraq adopted a "secure, engage, and build" strategy to develop the capacity and capability of local medical institutions in the city of Tal Afar. Over their year-long deployment, the unit was very successful in increasing the confidence of local Afghans in the legitimacy of their own government. Similarly, in 2010 in southern Afghanistan, 2nd Battalion, 1st Special Forces Group (Airborne) employed the MEDSEM concept as a way to connect local populations to their government and to the health officials responsible for their care while simultaneously addressing the health needs of the population. In both of these examples, medical operations succeeded because they were aligned with operational objectives and with the desired end state in a counterinsurgency environment. Unfortunately, these models of success were not quickly institutionalized into doctrine and training for the benefit of other units which followed. As a result, too many subsequent units engaged in medical operations which repeated the same mistakes over and over.

An assessment of the progress in Iraq and Afghanistan with health system reconstruction and development at the strategic level reveals that despite the multitude of difficulties initially, over time development conformed to some degree with the six

117

principles outlined in chapter 2. These principles include the need for a comprehensive systems-based approach, a focus on public health and primary care, the pursuit of equity, the development of capacity, remaining community-centered, and transitioning quickly from providing emergency health services to the development of a functional health system. In Iraq, the major shortcomings arose from deficiencies in adopting a systems-based approach, maintaining a focus on public health and primary care, and achieving equity. Afghanistan was overall more successful in conforming to all six principles, though significant inequality continued to exist, particularly between rural and urban areas.

Problems remained even years after the adoption of counterinsurgency tactics as there was no comprehensive program in Iraq or Afghanistan to ensure that all medical operations throughout the entirety of both countries were coordinated and aligned with counterinsurgency principles. Successful operations like the ones discussed in chapters four and five were too often the product of hard-charging and innovative Army medical personnel, rather than the result of a systems-based approach by Army medical leadership. In addition, there continued to be little connection between strategic planning in the capital and tactical operations at the local level. Too much of the approach to health system reconstruction and development was top-down rather than bottom-up. Interagency coordination also continued to be a major problem. Overall, there was not a complete transition from the conventional tactics which dominated early on to the irregular ones which proved to be more successful.

In the medical field, embracing the irregular tactics of counterinsurgency involved identifying those local populations most at risk and most vulnerable to insurgency, engaging them, and building relationships with them in conjunction with host nation medical officials via public health training and other forms of medical engagement. When done well, these types of medical operations accomplished the primary counterinsurgency objective: they fostered the development of effective governance by a legitimate government. However, some Army medical units continued to prioritize things like hospital-based training which, while not harmful, failed to engage the target population. As stated in FM 3-24, "the military forces that successfully defeat insurgencies are usually those able to overcome their institutional inclination to wage conventional war against insurgents."[2]

After 10 years of waging counterinsurgency in Iraq and Afghanistan and multiple repeated deployments by thousands of Army medical personnel involved in health system reconstruction and development, the Army Medical Department still has not developed training or doctrine on the subject of health system reconstruction and development while engaged in counterinsurgency. This is the case despite repeated calls to do so from Army medical personnel, particularly those with multiple deployments with operational units.

As outlined in chapter 3, some development theorists favor a severely circumscribed role for the U.S. Army in health system reconstruction and development during counterinsurgency. They believe that the Army should focus only on providing security, supporting military programs, and providing temporary emergency services when absolutely necessary. There are five main arguments given in support of this position:

> 1. The military lacks the configuration and the expertise to do development work well. As a result, its development efforts are consistently substandard.

2. The military focuses on short-term interventions at the expense of the development of sustainability and capacity over the long-term.

3. The military does not follow the lead of host nation health ministries because it has its own funding sources and hence develops its own programs.

4. Military activities are generally based on tactical or political goals rather than the principles of humanity, independence, impartiality, and equity which guide humanitarian workers.

5. Military involvement in health system reconstruction and development threatens the security of humanitarian workers.

The first three arguments were largely true of American involvement in Iraq and Afghanistan in the first several years after the end of major combat operations. However, over time U.S. Army medical personnel and PRTs learned from their mistakes and mainly stopped doing short-term projects in favor of longer term capacity-building efforts. With time, they also recognized the importance of host nation leadership over all medical programs. The experiences of U.S. Army medical personnel and PRTs validated the six principles for health system reconstruction and development discussed in chapter 3 which are based upon the experiences of humanitarian workers in developing countries over the last several decades.

As for the fourth argument, it remains true that military forces, unlike humanitarian workers, often seek to achieve tactical or political goals rather than simply promoting development for its own sake. Ultimately, though, military medical personnel share with humanitarian workers the goal of working with host nation personnel to build self-sufficient, functional, and sustainable health systems. The prioritization that military

120

forces use in getting to this goal may differ on occasion based upon tactical

considerations but ultimately the goal is the same. Experiences over the last 10 years

have impressed upon Army medical personnel the fact that short-term, ad hoc strategies

in the health sector inevitably fail and that only long-term strategies focused on building

capacity are successful. Finally, the concern on the part of NGOs and humanitarian

workers about their security when working with military forces in a counterinsurgency

environment is legitimate and military forces must do everything in their power to

mitigate these threats. Most importantly, military personnel need to recognize the

necessity of maintaining a division between "humanitarian space" and "military space"

and avoid blurring the distinction between the two.

Events in Iraq and Afghanistan demonstrate the folly of the idea held by some

development theorists that health system reconstruction and development in a

counterinsurgency environment could be successful without the significant involvement

of military medical personnel beyond simply providing security, aid to military programs,

and emergency care. In both Iraq and Afghanistan, analysis shows that there have been

two critical situations in which military involvement was essential for effective health

system reconstruction and development: immediately after the conclusion of major

combat operations and in unsecured areas not accessible to civilian organizations. The

initial months and then first several years following the conclusion of major combat

operations are a crucial period in the reconstruction and development of the host nation

health system. It is essential that organizations working with host nation officials engage

the population and begin the reconstruction process in a timely manner, particularly in

areas vulnerable to insurgency. Since it generally takes at least many months, if not more than a year, for most NGOs, international organizations, and other civilian organizations to establish a presence after major combat operations have ended, it almost inevitably falls on the military to perform this function until civilian organizations are in place.

Events over the last 10 years have shown the decisive role that security plays in counterinsurgency. A counterinsurgency force that is unable to secure the population is destined to be unsuccessful. In health system reconstruction and development, the degree of security in a given area is the primary determinant of which organizations and which strategies can be employed to engage the population in rebuilding the health system. A lack of security severely limits or completely eliminates the ability of civilian organizations to work in a given region. However, since these areas are often the base of the insurgency, it is essential that they not be written off as too difficult. Military forces, perhaps aligned with civilian organizations depending on the situation, have the ability to go into these areas, engage the population via effective medical operations aligned with counterinsurgency objectives and development principles, and create a more secure environment over time with space for civilian organizations to eventually operate. The ability of military units and medical personnel to perform this function in these crucial areas is essential to successful counterinsurgency.

There is absolutely no reason to believe, particularly given current budget concerns affecting the U.S. Government, that USAID and the State Department are going to vastly increase their expeditionary capacity and take over this dangerous mission, as some have called for. The failure in both Iraq and Afghanistan to engage the population and implement medical programs in key at-risk areas in the immediate aftermath of the conclusion of major combat operations created a hole which American forces and their

122

partners subsequently have spent many years trying to dig out of. Insecure areas are frequently the base of the insurgency and thus crucial ground for counterinsurgents to focus their efforts to improve governance and restore services, including health. Normally, only the military (sometimes partnered with civilian organizations) has the ability to go into these areas, live with the people and build relationships with them, creating space for host nation officials and civilians to operate.

The argument from development theorists that the involvement of military personnel in health system reconstruction and development should be severely restricted is not realistic, ignores the significance of the initial period after the conclusion of major combat operations before most civilian organizations are in place, and essentially writes off poor people living in insecure areas inaccessible to civilian organizations. On the other hand, the ISAF guidelines issued in Afghanistan in 2010 correctly prescribe the appropriate boundaries for military involvement in health system reconstruction and development. First, the host nation and its officials should always have the lead in all programs associated with health system reconstruction and all programs should have host nation professionals at the forefront. In addition, these programs should be host nation-owned, delivered to host nation standards, and sustainable over the long-term. Civilians should have primacy over health system reconstruction development and the military should be in a supporting role.

Development theorists critical of military involvement in health system reconstruction and development are ultimately short-sighted when assessing the military's role in Iraq and Afghanistan. Their criticisms concerning many of the Army's initial mistakes are apt, but these theorists ignore the progress made by Army medical personnel and units over the course of both wars. Army involvement in health system reconstruction and development is not forever destined to focus on expensive, short-term, and independently designed projects. Of course these types of operations are doomed to fail and Army medical personnel have largely learned that painful lesson. Over the course of the campaigns in both Iraq and Afghanistan, Army medical personnel moved away from these failed strategies and towards strategies which were based on both counterinsurgency and development principles. It is true that Army medical personnel still have plenty of room for improvement, but the evidence shows that they have to a significant degree learned from their initial mistakes and developed improved ways of supporting host nation officials. Development theorists are correct that Army medical personnel will never have the same level of expertise as civilians who spend their careers doing development work. For this reason, civilian experts should always maintain control over the process and have the lead role. But Army medical personnel play a crucial role during times and in situations where civilians are unable to act. The challenge for the Army Medical Department and Army medical personnel will be to continue to make progress by capturing lessons learned and incorporating them into training and doctrine.

As the events of the last 10 years demonstrate, achieving success in counterinsurgency is tremendously difficult. It is a protracted, messy, and confusing form of warfare. The medical aspect of counterinsurgency requires not only effective planning at the national level but more importantly extended engagement with the population, alongside host nation health officials and providers at the local level. It is essential that these engagements are focused on insecure areas where the insurgency is strongest in order to be to be effective. Success requires the Army Medical Department and all its physicians, physician assistants, nurses, medics, and other medical professionals to be completely engaged. There is no way that the U.S. Army can succeed in the tremendously difficult and complex business of counterinsurgency without a complete commitment from the Army Medical Department and all its personnel (along with all other Army branches) to do everything in their power to achieve success. In a counterinsurgency, the Army Medical Department is obligated to go beyond its primary mission, conserving the fighting strength of American forces, to take on the secondary task of host nation health system reconstruction and development. The U.S. Army has been engaged in large-scale counterinsurgency operations (Vietnam, Iraq, Afghanistan) for approximately 20 of the last 50 years and has provided support to smaller counterinsurgency operations in places like Central America, for many of the intervening years. Though in the near future U.S. forces may "no longer be sized to conduct large-scale, prolonged stability operations" as stated in the 2012 Defense Strategic Guidance, it remains highly likely that the U.S. Army will continue to be involved in some form of counterinsurgency in the future.[3] It may involve simply providing support to governments at risk to prevent small conflicts from developing into full-scale counterinsurgencies. The Army Medical Department cannot afford to repeat the mistakes made after Vietnam, in which lessons learned under difficult conditions on the battlefield about counterinsurgency operations were not effectively captured and institutionalized in doctrine and training.

Recommendations

1. The Army Medical Department should develop doctrine and training for health system reconstruction and development while engaged in counterinsurgency. This

doctrine should include lessons learned from Army experiences throughout history, up to and including Iraq and Afghanistan. It should particularly address the complexities of integrating and synchronizing all civilian, military, and host nation organizations involved in health system reconstruction and development. It should also reflect knowledge gained from health system development by civilian organizations around the world. Most importantly, this doctrine should be based upon a careful and comprehensive analysis at the tactical, operational, and strategic levels addressing which methods have worked and which have not. Training on health system reconstruction and development in counterinsurgency should be integrated into all levels of Army Medical Department education including the Basic Officer Leader Course and the Captain's Career Course. It should also be incorporated into Joint Readiness Training Center and National Training Center scenarios where commanders will benefit from learning about the harm of direct patient care by American forces in many situations and the benefits of a strategy focused on capacity building and improving local governance. It is absolutely essential that the Army Medical Department does not repeat the mistake made after Vietnam in failing to institutionalize lessons learned by Army medical personnel under some very demanding conditions on bloody battlefields.

2. Mechanisms to improve the integration, coordination, and synchronization of all military and civilian organizations involved in health system reconstruction and development at both the strategic and operational levels should be developed. The failure to successfully integrate the various civilian and military organizations involved in Iraq and Afghanistan's health system reconstruction and development, which began in the pre-conflict planning stages and continued nearly unabated throughout years of conflict,

resulted in recurrent duplication of effort and tremendous inefficiency. Multiple books and articles have been written concerning the failures in interagency coordination throughout all aspects of government involvement in Iraq and Afghanistan. Many of the solutions proposed and executed thus far have not succeeded, illustrating the scope and complexity of the problem. In the health sector, it is absolutely essential that there be an operational level mechanism for bringing together all U.S. Government civilian and military organizations as well as other key stakeholders including host nation officials, NGOs, and international organizations in order to develop strategic plans and objectives, set priorities, and integrate programs. The way in which PRTs overcame their initial missteps and succeeded to a significant degree in integrating civilian and military organizations at the tactical level can serve as an effective model for civilian and military integration in health system reconstruction and development. In addition, there needs to be unity of effort among groups working on reconstruction and development of both the military and civilian health systems in order to ensure that the appropriate prioritization is given to each and that programs are implemented which are complementary and beneficial to both.

3. The Army Medical Department should develop an International Health Program. The DOD Office of Force Health Protection currently has an International Health Division which develops policies concerning all aspects of military involvement in global health. The Army should develop a program focused more at the operational level, given the fact that it provides the physicians, nurses, and other medical personnel who do the majority of the work on the ground in difficult conditions around the globe.[4] This International Health Program should not be limited to health system reconstruction

and development in counterinsurgency, but should also include stability operations, humanitarian assistance, disaster relief, and any setting involving international health. This office would be responsible for overseeing the development of doctrine and training concerning international health and would also seek to build long-term relationships with NGOs and international organizations.

4. The PRT medical section should be expanded. PRTs in Iraq and Afghanistan have accomplished many positive things over the last several years after some initial difficulties. Overall, they are a successful example of civilian and military integration among the crowd of failures. The makeup of the medical section of PRTs varied across Iraq and Afghanistan but in both cases there was not sufficient staffing to accomplish the mission. PRTs should include a medical provider who is a Field Grade Officer and a Medical Service Corps Officer to coordinate and oversee all aspects of programming and logistics, in addition to the physician assistant, Non-Commissioned Officer, and two medics currently on the team. Furthermore, pre-deployment training focused on the principles of health system reconstruction and development as well as cultural awareness should be developed for PRTs.

5. All medical operations in a counterinsurgency should be aligned with operational objectives and consistent with counterinsurgency principles. Medical programs undertaken during counterinsurgency should always seek to connect the population with their local health officials and providers and to develop the confidence of the population that their government and health ministry are interested in their care. Like all counterinsurgency operations, counterinsurgency medical operations should seek the

development of effective governance. Whenever possible, these medical programs should seek to target the populations most at risk and most vulnerable to insurgents.

6. Health system reconstruction and development undertaken during counterinsurgency should adhere to established principles for effective development. These principles include those found in civilian development literature as well as those derived from military experiences. They include the 6 principles outlined in chapter 3: taking a comprehensive systems-based approach, focusing on public health and primary care, striving for an equitable system which minimizes disparities, enhancing the development of capacity, remaining community-centered, and moving quickly from providing emergency health services to developing a functional health system. In addition, all projects should be host nation-led, appropriate to the standards of a developing country, affordable in the long-term, and sustainable. Low cost and small footprint approaches are preferred over expensive and unsustainable projects. The U.S.-funded multimillion dollar high-end projects which were commonplace in Iraq and Afghanistan and which failed because they were neither appropriate nor desired by host nation officials have no place in effective health system reconstruction and development.

Measures of effectiveness which account for both medical effects and other important counterinsurgency-based lines of operation including security, information operations, and governance should be developed and tracked for all medical operations. Finally, health system reconstruction and development involves the transfer of information, respect, and knowledge in multiple directions and both counterinsurgency forces and host nation personnel have much to gain from the other. U.S. Army medical personnel certainly do not have all the answers and have much to learn from working side-by-side with host nation officials, providers, and citizens to experience first-hand some of the different methods and approaches employed successfully in other countries.

The Way Ahead

U.S. Army medical personnel involved in health system reconstruction and development during counterinsurgency have the opportunity to play a powerful role in overall mission success via support for host nation officials and governments in building more effective public health programs and providing basic health care to millions of the medically underserved. These efforts can potentially save thousands of lives while simultaneously empowering masses of people in war torn countries to take charge of their own affairs and their own governments. Future success requires the abandonment of failed strategies and the adoption of methods proven effective. It also requires continuous analysis and education, including learning from the experiences of humanitarian organizations involved in health system reconstruction and development throughout the developing world.

Further research in the following areas has the potential to aid future Army efforts in health system reconstruction and development during counterinsurgency:

1. The appropriate metrics to quantify the success or failure of medical operations.

2. Ways to improve working relationships between NGOs and Army units.

3. Mechanisms for better integrating civilian and military organizations involved in health system reconstruction and development.

4. Evidence to support or refute the notion that health system reconstruction and development is a significant contributor to security and nation building.

[1]Headquarters, Department of the Army, Field Manual 3-24, *Counterinsurgency,* 1-26.

[2]Ibid., ix.

[3]Department of Defense, *Sustaining U.S. Government Leadership: Priorities for 21st Century Defense* (Washington, DC: Government Printing Office, 2012).

[4]The U.S. Army's Long Term Health Education Training program includes an option to pursue a Masters of Public Health in International Health and Policy Management. However, currently graduates of this program generally have little or no involvement with the development of doctrine and training concerning international health.

BIBLIOGRAPHY

Books

Gates, John Morgan. *Schoolbooks and Krags, The United States Army in the Philippines, 1898-1902*. Westport, CT: Greenwood Press, 1973.

Jones, Seth G. *In the Graveyard of Empires: America's War in Afghanistan*. New York: W.W. Norton and Company, 2009.

Sen, Amartya. *Development as Freedom*. New York: Anchor Books, 2000.

Special Inspector General for Iraq Reconstruction. *Hard Lessons: The Iraq Reconstruction Experience*. Washington, DC: U.S. Independent Agencies and Commissions, 2009.

Tamas, Andy. *Warriors and Nation Builders: Development and the Military in Afghanistan*. Kingston, Ontario: Canadian Defense Academy Press, 2009.

Wilensky, Robert J. *Military Medicine to Win Hearts and Minds: Aid to Civilians in the Vietnam War*. Lubbock, TX: Texas Tech University Press, 2004.

Periodicals

Alderman, Shawn, Jon Christensen, and Ingrham Crawford. "Medical Seminars: A New Paradigm for SOF Counterinsurgency Medical Programs." *Journal of Special Operations Medicine* 10, no. 1 (Winter 2010): 16-22.

Baker, Jay. "Medical Diplomacy in Full Spectrum Operations." *Military Review* (September/October 2007): 67-73.

Burkle Jr., Frederick M., Bradley A. Woodruff, and Eric K. Noji. "Lessons and Controversies: Planning and Executing Immediate Relief in the Aftermath of the War in Iraq." *Third World Quarterly* 26 (2005): 797-814. http://www.jstor.org/discover/10.2307/3993721?uid=3739672&uid=2129&uid=2134&uid=2&uid=70&uid=4&uid=3739256&sid=56108111593 (accessed 11 February 2012).

Feil, Scott. "Building Better Foundations: Security in Postconflict Reconstruction." *Washington Quarterly* 25, no. 4 (Autumn 2002): 97-109.

Hamid, Simon. "Guidelines for Implementing Medical Operations in the Counterinsurgency Fight: A Framework for Engagement." *Journal of Special Operations Medicine* 11 no. 2 (Spring 2011): 7-11.

Himmler, Bruno. "Health Care Diplomacy: The Iraq Experience and How It Can Shape the Future." *Military Medicine* (December 2009): 15-23.

Laipson, Ellen B. "Information-Sharing in Conflict Zones: Can the USG and the NGOs Do More?" *Studies in Intelligence* 49, no. 4 (2005): 55-64. https://www.cia.gov/ library/center-for-the-study-of-intelligence/csi-publications/csi-studies/ studies/vol49no4/USG_NGOs_5.htm (accessed 3 May 2012).

Loevinsohn, Benjamin, and Ghulam Dastagir Sayed. "Lessons from the Health Sector in Afghanistan: How Progress Can Be Made in Challenging Circumstances." *JAMA* 300, no. 6 (August 2008): 724-726.

Lynn, David C., and Robert A. De Lorenzo. "Advising and Assisting an Iraqi Army Medical Clinic: Observations of a U.S. Military Support Mission." *Military Medicine* 176 (September 2011): 998-1002.

Murphy, Sean, and Dean Agner. "Cooperative Health Engagement in Stability Operations and Expanding Partner Capability and Capacity." *Military Medicine* 174, no. 8 (August 2009): 3-7.

Petraeus, David. "Multinational Force–Iraq Commander's Counterinsurgency Guidance." *Military Review* (September-October 2008). http://usacac.army.mil/CAC2/ MilitaryReview/Archives/English/MilitaryReview_20081031_art004.pdf (accessed 5 May 2012).

Stone, Blake. "Blind Ambition: Lessons Learned and Not Learned in an Embedded PRT." *Prism* 1, no. 4 (September 2010): 147-158. http://www.ndu.edu/ press/lib/images/prism1-4/Prism_147-158_Stone.pdf (accessed 29 April 2012).

Thompson, Donald F. "The Role of Medical Diplomacy in Stabilizing Afghanistan." *Defense Horizons,* no. 63 (May 2008): 1-8.

Webster, Paul C. "Iraq's health system yet to heal from ravages of war." *The Lancet* 378, no. 9794 (September 2011): 863-866.

Government Documents

Chairman, Joint Chiefs of Staff. Joint Publication (JP) 1-02, *Department of Defense Dictionary of Military and Associated Terms.* Washington, DC: Government Printing Office, 2010.

———. Joint Publication (JP) 3-07, *Stability Operations.* Washington, DC: Government Printing Office, 2011.

———.Joint Publication (JP) 3-29, *Foreign Humanitarian Assistance.* Washington, DC: Government Printing Office, 2009.

————. Joint Publication (JP) 3-57, *Civil-Military Operations*. Washington, DC: Government Printing Office, 2008.

————. Joint Publication (JP) 4-02, *Health Service Support*. Washington, DC: Government Printing Office, 31 October 2006.

————. Joint Publication (JP) 3-29, *Foreign Humanitarian Assistance*. Washington, DC: Government Printing Office, 2009.

Department of Defense. Department of Defense Instruction (DoDI) 2205.02, *Humanitarian and Civic Assistance (HCA) Activities*. Washington, DC: Government Printing Office, 2008.

————. Department of Defense Instruction (DoDI) 3000.05, *Stability Operations*. Washington, DC: Government Printing Office, 16 September 2009.

————. Department of Defense Instruction (DoDI) 6000.16, *Military Health Support for Stability Operations*. Washington, DC: Government Printing Office, 17 May 2010.

————. *Sustaining U.S. Government Leadership: Priorities for 21st Century Defense*. Washington, DC: Government Printing Office, 2012.

Headquarters, Department of the Army. Army Tactics, Techniques, and Procedures (ATTP) 4-02, *Army Health System*. Washington, DC: Government Printing Office, October 2011.

————. Field Manual (FM) 3-0, *Operations*. Washington, DC: Government Printing Office, February 2011.

————. Field Manual (FM) 3-07, *Stability Operations*. Washington, DC: Government Printing Office, October 2008.

————. Field Manual (FM) 3-24, *Counterinsurgency*. Washington, DC: Government Printing Office, December 2006.

————. Field Manual (FM) 3-24.2, *Tactics in Counterinsurgency*. Washington, DC: Government Printing Office, April 2009.

————. Field Manual (FM) 8-42, *Combat Health Support in Stability Operations and Support Operations*. Washington, DC: Government Printing Office, October 1997.

Other Sources

Abbaszadeh, Nina, Mark Crow, Marianne El-Khoury, Jonathan Gandomi, David Kuwayama, Christopher MacPherson, Meghan Nutting, Nealin Parker, and Taya Weiss. "Provincial Reconstruction Teams: Lessons and Recommendations." Princeton University Woodrow Wilson School of Public and International Affairs, January 2008. http://wws.princeton.edu/research/pwreports_f07/ wws591b.pdf (accessed 29 April 2012).

Ackermann, Bret T. "Assisting Host Nations in Developing Health Systems." Strategy Research Project, U.S. Army War College, 2010. http://www.dtic.mil/cgi-bin/ GetTRDoc?AD= ADA522017 (accessed 5 May 2012).

Afghan Public Health Institute Ministry of Public Health. "Afghanistan Mortality Survey 2010." November 2011. http://measuredhs.com/pubs/pdf/FR248/FR248.pdf (accessed 2 May 2012).

Armstrong, Kimberly K. "Army Medical Department Support to Stability Operations." Strategy Research Project, U.S. Army War College, 2007. http://www.dtic.mil/ cgi-bin/GetTRDoc?AD=ada469380 (accessed 15 April 2012).

Bebber, Robert J. "The Role of Provincial Reconstruction Teams in Counterinsurgency Operations: Khost Province, Afghanistan." *Small Wars Journal* (10 November 2008). http://smallwarsjournal.com/blog/journal/docs-temp/131-bebber.pdf?q=mag/docs-temp/131-bebber.pdf (accessed 2 May 2012).

Bennis, Phyllis, Martha Honey, and Stephen Zunes. "The Failure of U.S. Policy toward Iraq and Proposed Alternatives." *Foreign Policy in Focus* (1 June 2001). http://www.fpif.org/articles/the_failure_of_us_policy_toward_iraq_and_proposed _alternatives (accessed 29 April 2012).

Bricknell, MCM. "Reflections on medical aspects of ISAF IX in Afghanistan." *JR Army Med Corps* 153, no. 1 (March 2007): 44-51.

Bryan, Edward L. "Medical Engagement: Beyond the MEDCAP." Monograph, School of Advanced Military Studies, U.S. Army Command and General Staff College, 2008. http://www.dtic.mil/cgi-bin/GetTRDoc?AD=ADA485508 (accessed 5 May 2012).

Bundt, Thomas S. "Synchronizing U.S. Government Efforts toward Collaborative Healthcare Policymaking in Iraq." Strategic Studies Institute, U.S. Army War College, March 2010. http://www.strategicstudiesinstitute.army.mil/pubs/ display.cfm?pubid=978 (accessed 29 April 2012).

Center for Army Lessons Learned. *PRT Playbook.* No. 07-34, September 2007.

Center for Economic and Social Rights. "The Human Costs of War in Iraq." 2003. http://www.cesr.org/downloads/Human%20Costs%20of%20War%20in%20 Iraq.pdf (accessed 29 April 2012).

CJTF-82. "Key Lessons Learned." 2008. http://lessonslearned.amedd.army.mil/ (accessed 11 February 2012).

———. " Surgeon AAR." 2008. http://lessonslearned.amedd.army.mil/ (accessed 11 February 2012).

CJTF-82 Surgeon's Section. "Information Paper: CJTF-82 Health Sector Development in Afghanistan." 3 March 2008. http://lessonslearned.amedd.army.mil/ (accessed 11 February 2012).

Cornish, Stephen, and Marit Glad. "Civil-military Relations: No Room for Humanitarianism in Comprehensive Approaches." *Security Policy Library*, 5-2008. http://reliefweb.int/node/24781 (accessed 5 May 2012).

Dalil, Suraya. "On the Road to Recovery." USAID in the News, 13 December 2011. http://afghanistan.usaid.gov/en/USAID/Article/2584/On_the_road_to_recovery (accessed 5 May 2012).

Federal News Service. "Department of Defense Bloggers Roundtable with COL Schuyler K. Geller, Command Surgeon and Commander, Medical Training Advisory Group, Camp Eggers, NATO Training Mission-Afghanistan/Combined Security Transition Command-Afghanistan." 23 June 2010. http://www.defense.gov/ Blog_files/Blog_assets/ 20100623_schuyler2_transcript.pdf (accessed 2 May 2012).

Gimble, Thomas F. "Principal Deputy Inspector General Department of Defense before the House Oversight and Government Reform Committee Subcommittee on National Security and Foreign Affairs: DoD IG Assessment of Arms, Ammunition, and Explosives Control and Accountability; Security Assistance; and Sustainment for the Afghan National Security Forces." 12 February 2009. http://www.dodig.mil/ IGInformation/ Speeches/HOGR%202-12-09.pdf (accessed 2 May 2012).

Hanlin, Rory. "One Team's Approach to Village Stability Operations." *Small Wars Journal* (4 September 2011). http://smallwarsjournal.com/node/11412 (accessed 2 May 2012).

Headquarters, International Security Assistance Force. "ISAF Guidance on Military Medical Engagement in Health Sector Reconstruction and Development." 28 July 2010.

Health and Fragile States Network. "Health Systems Strengthening in Fragile Contexts: A Report on Good Practices and New Approaches." June 2009. http://www.bsf-south-sudan.org/sites/default/files/Good_Practice_Report_final.pdf (accessed 29 April 2012).

Himmler, Bruno. "Humanitarian Assistance and Capacity Development: Unifying Efforts of DoD and the Civilian Community." *Peacekeeping and Stability Operations Institute (PKSOI) Bulletin* 2, no. 3 (April 2010). http://pksoi.army.mil/PKM/ publications/bulletin/volume2issue3/humanitarian.cfm (accessed 3 May 2012).

International Security Assistance Force. *ISAF PRT Handbook*, 4th ed. 2009. https://www.cimicweb.org/Lists/PRT%20Handbook/AllItems.aspx (accessed 2 May 2012).

Islamic Republic of Afghanistan Ministry of Public Health. "A Basic Package of Health Services for Afghanistan, 2005/1384." http://www.msh.org/afghanistan/pdf/ Afghanistan_BPHS_2005_1384.pdf (accessed 2 May 2012).

Jackson, Ashley. *Quick Impact, Quick Collapse: The Dangers of Militarized Aid in Afghanistan,* January 2010. http://www.scribd.com/doc/25889897/Oxfam-Quick-Impact-Quick-Collapse (accessed 29 April 2012).

Jawad (AL-ainachi) Shakir, Maysaa Mahmood, Ali Al Ameri, and Gregg Nakano. "Post-Conflict Reconstruction in the Health Sector: Host Nation Perspective." In *Transitions: Issues, Challenges and Solutions in International Assistance*, edited by Henry R. Yarger, 95-110. November 2010. http://www.dtic.mil/cgi-bin/GetTRDoc?AD=ADA548963 (accessed 25 April 2012).

Jones, Seth G., Lee H. Hilborne, C. Ross Anthony, Lois M. Davis, Federico Girosi, Cheryl Benard, Rachel M. Swanger, Anita Datar Garten, and Anga Timilsina. *Health System Reconstruction and Nation-Building.* Santa Monica, CA: RAND Corporation, Center for Domestic and International Health Security, 2007. http://www.rand.org/pubs/research_briefs/ 2007/RAND_RB9237.html (accessed 14 April 2012).

—. *Securing Health: Lessons from Nation-Building Missions.* Santa Monica, CA: RAND Corporation, Center for Domestic and International Health Security, 2006. http://www.rand.org/pubs/ monographs/2006/RAND_MG321.pdf (accessed 14 April 2012).

Headquarters, 30th Medical Brigade. "Operation Iraqi Freedom 05-07 After Action Review." http://lessonslearned.amedd.army.mil (accessed 11 February 2012).

Krane, Jim. "New U.S. Commander to Change Iraq Focus." Iraq Updates, 31 January 2006. http://admin.iraqupdates.net/p_articles.php/article/5192 (accessed 5 May 2012).

Lawrence, Quil. "Gains in Afghan Health: Too Good to be True?" *National Public Radio* 17 January 2012. http://www.npr.org/2012/01/17/145338803/gains-in-afghan-health-too-good-to-be-true (accessed 2 May 2012).

Malsby III, Robert F. "Into Which End does the Thermometer Go? Application of Military Medicine in Counterinsurgency: Does Direct Patient Care by American Service Members Work?" Master's Thesis, Command and General Staff College, Ft Leavenworth, KS, 2008. http://www.dtic.mil/cgi-bin/GetTRDoc?AD=ADA 501911 (accessed 5 May 2012).

Messineo, Carol. "The United States Military as an Agent of Development: Counterinsurgency Doctrine and Development Assistance." International Affairs Working Paper 2010-05, October 2010. http://www.gpia.info/files/u706/Messineo_2010-05.pdf (accessed 3 May 2012).

Naland, John K. "Lessons from Embedded Provincial Reconstruction Teams in Iraq." United States Institute of Peace Special Report, October 2011. http://www.usip.org/files/resources/SR290.pdf (accessed 1 May 2012).

National Public Radio. "Following the reconstruction money in Iraq." 30 August 2010. http://www.npr.org/templates/story/story.php?storyId=129535004 (accessed 1 May 2012).

Wilton Park. "Winning Hearts and Minds in Afghanistan: Assessing the Effectiveness of Development and Operations." Wilton Park Conference, 11 March–14 March 2010. http://www.eisf.eu/resources/library/1004WPCReport.pdf (accessed 2 May 2012).

Rubenstein, Leonard S. "Health Initiatives and Counter-Insurgency Strategy in Afghanistan." United States Institute of Peace Brief, 5 March 2010. http://www.usip.org/files/resources/PB%2012%20Health%20Initiatives%20and%20Counterinsurgency%20Strategy%20in%20Afghanistan.pdf (accessed 29 April 2011).

———. "Post Conflict Health Reconstruction: New Foundations for U.S. Policy." United States Institute of Peace Working Paper, September 2009. http://www.usip.org/files/resources/post-conflict_health_reconstruction.pdf (accessed 25 April 2012).

Small Wars Journal Editors. "ISAF Counterinsurgency Guidance Released." *Small Wars Journal,* 25 August 2009. http://smallwarsjournal.com/blog/isaf-counterinsurgency-guidance-released (accessed 2 May 2012).

Smith, David J. "Health Sector Reconstruction and Development in ISAF." ISAF HQ, Kabul, Afghanistan. 4 October 2011. http://95.110.200.129/act/images/stories/events/2011/medconf/d1_smith.pdf (accessed 2 May 2012).

Stoddard, Abby, Adele Harmer, and Victoria DiDomenico. "Providing aid in insecure environments: 2009 Update." Humanitarian Policy Group Policy Brief 34, April 2009. http://www.odi.org.uk/resources/docs/4243.pdf (accessed 1 May 2012).

Swanson, Robert C., Annette Bongiovanni, Elizabeth Bradley, Varnee Murugan, Jesper Sundewall, Arvind Betigeri, Frank Nyonator, Adriano Cattaneo, Brandi Harless, Andrey Ostrovsky, and Ronald Labonté. "Toward a consensus on guiding principles for health systems strengthening." *PLoS Med* 7, no. 12 (December 2010). http://www.plosmedicine.org/article/info:doi/10.1371/journal.pmed. 1000385 (accessed 29 April 2012).

Tarantino Jr., David A., and Shakir Jawad. "Iraq Health Sector Reconstruction: An After-Action Review." Uniformed Services University of the Health Sciences, 9-11 January 2007. http://csis.org/images/stories/globalhealth/Iraq%20AAR%20final% 201%20OCT.pdf (accessed 29 April 2012).

UNICEF and Central Statistics Office, Afghanistan Transitional Authority. "Multiple indicator cluster survey 2003 report for Afghanistan." http://www.childinfo.org/ mics2_afghanistan.html (accessed 2 May 2012).

United Nations. "United Nations General Assembly Resolution 46/182," 19 December 1991. http://ochaonline.un.org/cap2006/webpage.asp?Page=1951 (accessed 29 April 2012).

United States Agency for International Development (USAID). *Sustaining Health Gains–Building Systems*. Washington, DC: USAID, October 2009. http://pdf.usaid.gov/ pdf_docs/PDACN511.pdf (accessed 11 April 2012).

U.S. Army Medical Department Lessons Learned. "Discussion on Civil-Military Operations: Division Surgeons Community of Practice." October-December 2004. http://lessonslearned .amedd.army.mil/ (accessed 11 February 2012).

U.S. House of Representatives. Committee on Armed Services, Subcommittee on Oversight and Investigations. "Agency Stovepipes versus Strategic Agility: Lessons We Need to Learn from Provincial Reconstruction Teams in Iraq and Afghanistan." April 2008. http://democrats.armedservices.house.gov/ index.cfm/files/serve?File_id=20ca518e-0183-433f-be5a-7e872dbc41b7 (accessed 1 May 2012).

World Health Organization (WHO). *Everybody's Business: Strengthening Health Systems To Improve Health Outcomes Who's Framework For Action*. Geneva, Switzerland: WHO Press, 2007. http://www.who.int/healthsystems/strategy/ everybodys_business.pdf (accessed 5 May 2012).

———. *Monitoring the Building Blocks of Health Systems: A Handbook of Indicators and Their Measurement Strategies*. Geneva, Switzerland: WHO Press, 2010.

http://www.who.int/ healthinfo/systems/WHO_MBHSS_2010_full_web.pdf (accessed 5 May 2012).

———. *World Health Statistics 2011.* Geneva, Switzerland: WHO Press, 2010. http://www.who.int/whosis/whostat/EN_WHS2011_Full.pdf (accessed 5 May 2012).

———. "World Health Statistics 2010 Indicator Compendium Interim Version." http://www.who.int/whosis/indicators/WHS10_IndicatorCompendium_20100513. pdf (accessed 5 May 2012).

World Health Organization. Eastern Mediterranean Regional Office (EMRO). "Health Systems Profile: Iraq." 2005. http://www.emro.who.int/iraq/pdf/Health SystemsProfile.pdf (accessed 29 April 2012).